APPLIED
VISUAL
MERCHANDISING

APPLIED
VISUAL
MERCHANDISING

kenneth h. mills
Gateway Technical Institute

judith e. paul
Assistant Professor of Business Administration
University of Wisconsin

Prentice-Hall, Inc., Englewood Cliffs, New Jersey 07632

Library of Congress Cataloging in Publication Data

MILLS, KENNETH H.
    Applied visual merchandising.

    Rev. ed. of: Create distinctive displays. 1974.
    Bibliography: p.
    Includes index.
    1. Display of merchandise. I. Paul, Judith E.,
1939–   II. Title.
HF5845.M54—1982   659.1'5   81-15322
ISBN 0-13-043331-4   AACR2

Editorial/production supervision and interior design by Pamela Wilder
Cover design by Mark A. Binn
Cover photograph by Stan Wakefield
Manufacturing buyer: Ed O'Dougherty

Previously published under the title *Create Distinctive Displays*

Printed in the United States of America
10 9 8 7 6 5 4 3 2 1

ISBN 0-13-043331-4

Prentice-Hall International, Inc., *London*
Prentice-Hall of Australia Pty. Limited, *Sydney*
Prentice-Hall of Canada, Ltd., *Toronto*
Prentice-Hall of India Private Limited, *New Delhi*
Prentice-Hall of Japan, Inc., *Tokyo*
Prentice-Hall of Southeast Asia Pte. Ltd., *Singapore*
Whitehall Books Limited, *Wellington, New Zealand*

JUDITH E. PAUL

To my parents, Mr. and Mrs. Arthur Edison, whose regard for the educational process and enthusiastic support of all young people served as an inspiration to me throughout my life. Through their consistent encouragement, warmth, and understanding, they gave me the desire to foster creative learning in others, as they had fostered mine.

KENNETH H. MILLS

The contents of this text were developed and inspired over the years with the assistance of students and colleagues. However, the text itself was brought to fruition only with the continued support and love of my wife Darlene.

The authors jointly offer their appreciation to Sandra Stickrod for her efforts in assisting in the preparation of an accurate and complete manuscript.

Contents

5 **THE DESIGN PRINCIPLES OF BALANCE AND EMPHASIS   37**

6 **THE DESIGN PRINCIPLES OF HARMONY, PROPORTION, AND RHYTHM   46**

7 **COLOR: THE LIFE OF A DISPLAY   60**

8 **GUIDELINES TO LIGHTING   75**

9 **PROMOTIONAL AND INSTITUTIONAL DISPLAYS: THEORY AND APPLICATION   90**

10 **VISUAL MERCHANDISING POLICIES AND PROCEDURES: PEOPLE/PROCESSES/IDEAS   99**

Preface

Visual merchandising is a sales-supporting activity. It is an aspect of merchandising in which every window and shelf is a stage, and where the visual merchandise director, visual merchandise staff, and sales promotion director are presented with situations demanding enormous creativity in the use of theatrical and merchandising principles. Visual merchandising, therefore, involves much more than ornamentation. Visual selling—merchandise presentation in window and interior display—is responsible for one out of every four retail sales. It is the visual merchandise director and his staff who give shape and substance to this vital force in retail merchandising.

The visual merchandise person's chief responsibility is to help the store increase its sales by effectively using store windows and showcases to display merchandise. It is estimated that the average pedestrian spends less than 11 seconds looking in each store window he passes, so it is essential that displays have immediate impact in conveying the type, quality, and uses of the goods for sale.

The visual merchandise person's specific duties depend largely on the type and size of the establishment for which he works. In a large store, his duties may consist solely of creating of ideas, drawing sketches, and supervising other workers in making props and setting up the display. In smaller stores, he may not only originate the idea but also carry it out in detail, right down to carpentry, remodeling old equipment, and so forth. A display person may also be self-employed and freelance his services, or work for a wholesaler.

Many individuals in the merchandising area are confronted with the need for a knowledge of display, regardless of their specific job titles. The retail buyer will select merchandise to be displayed from his or her department and often will be responsible for replacing items purchased from floor or window displays. The fashion coordinator will also be involved with the display department, as will the advertising department. Therefore, it is essential that all merchandisers have a practical working knowledge of the purpose and functions of display so they may better present merchandise to the consumer.

It will be noted that throughout this text the practical application of display is stressed through a gradual building process. The text should be supplemented with knowledge gained through working with fellow students, giving demonstrations, creating displays, and contacting leading business-people in the community. This well-rounded approach to display is necessary for any person interested in management as his or her future goal, as well as for the person wishing to pursue a career as a professional display person. Such positions as freelance display person and display department head may require the individual to gain additional professional and educational experience, but this book provides a basic theoretical and practical foundation upon which to build.

The visual merchandising student, as a result of mastering the materials in this text will become proficient in the following competencies:

Understand the several components of display

Analyze and evaluate the various types of displays

Understand the principles of color, lighting, and design

Construct both hard-line and soft-line displays which are effective at selling merchandise

Design, lay out, and produce showcards

Define and use visual merchandising terminology appropriately

Select appropriate props for a given display

Understand the place that visual merchandising has in a store, a department, or a corporation

The final goal, then, of the study of merchandise display is to provide the individual with the knowledge, skills, and understanding that will enable him or her to arrange a functionally effective display area. This display area should attract the customer's eye, induce her or him to enter the store, approach the merchandiser, and say, "Wrap it up, please."

It is the feeling of the authors that an individual following the methods and procedures set forth in this text will be prepared for the occupational goal.

The October 1968 issue of *Display World* describes a program using the materials, principles, and procedures included in this text.

Kenneth H. Mills
Judith E. Paul

APPLIED VISUAL MERCHANDISING

1

Introduction to Visual Merchandising

Visual merchandising is the presentation of a store and its merchandise to the customer through the teamwork of advertising, display, special events, fashion coordination, and merchandising in order to sell the goods and services offered by the store. Neither advertising, nor display, nor special events, nor fashion coordination, nor merchandising can function alone; all must be combined into a single team with one aim—to sell the goods and services offered by the store.

Particular emphasis must be placed on the necessity for coordination between the advertising function and the display function, two of the most important aspects of the various sales-supporting functions in a merchandising establishment. Advertising is usually planned well in advance of its presentation, as are some of the major seasonal displays. Advertising themes and campaigns must be backed up by interior and exterior displays, and the creators of both must be certain that the media space purchased and the display space used have been profitable.

Another factor requiring emphasis is the merchandise being promoted. Because complete coordination is necessary among copywriters, buyers, artists, and display people, all of them must be acquainted with the merchandise firsthand. There is no better way to lose customer confidence than to presell merchandise and then have the customer find that it isn't as he or she was led to believe.

FIVE STEPS OF A SALE

Visual merchandising must sell. It can do this most effectively when all the principles of design and arrangement are employed intelligently. This is possible only if the display person fully understands these principles and, by applying them, leads the customer through the five steps of a sale with the display. These five steps are:

1. Attract the attention of the passerby.
2. Arouse his or her interest.
3. Create desire.
4. Win confidence to give the customer faith in the store and product.
5. Cause the decision to buy (the customer, barriers broken down, makes the purchase).

Courtesy of Gimbels Midwest, Inc., Milwaukee, Wis.

FIGURE 1–1 *The purpose of visual merchandising is to sell the goods and services of the store*

ATTRACT ATTENTION

Visual merchandising must *attract* and *hold* the passerby until interest is aroused. A display may bring a person over from a block away, yet lack the quality to arouse interest in the merchandise displayed.

How does display attract attention? Various methods may be used to provide the attraction, but it is difficult to select and apply the appropriate one.

If a display is sufficently surprising and unusual, a potential customer will cross the street to view it more closely. It makes no difference whether this result is achieved by movement, color, lighting, form, or lettering. *Contrast* especially can be relied on to attract the attention of a maximum number of passersby. Any method may be used as long as it does not evoke any disapproval or conflict in the observer's mind.

AROUSE INTEREST

In display, the observer's mental process is directed systematically toward the target. For the most part, passersby approach windows without purpose. Attention is arrested by something positive, some striking point that we will term the focus, or optical center, of the display. This focus may be created by lighting, movement, color, or the merchandise itself. From there, the eye of the observer will move in the desired direction through the display by use of devices such as arrows—subtle or definite—that lead to the salable merchandise.

Observation should be guided along lines easy to follow: from decoration, to merchandise, to showcard, and finally, to the price tag. Use quality effects and make every attempt to create a favorable reaction in the mind of the potential customer.

CREATE DESIRE

The consumer must be made to want the product; this desire can be aroused in the following ways:

1. Demonstrate the qualities and benefits of the product.
2. Demonstrate the use of the product.
3. Present the product in such a way as to increase the possibility of inducing a sale. It is not sufficient just to please the observer; the objective is to sell the merchandise. Therefore, an impulsive desire for the merchandise must be aroused. Explain the necessity of the product, show its advantages, and win the potential customer's confidence in the establishment's firm faith in the product.
4. Sell the idea that the article is exactly what the spectator needs and that owning this article will bring complete satisfaction.

WIN CONFIDENCE

Tell the truth about the product, bringing out the safe and economical characteristics of both the store and the product.

CAUSE DECISION TO BUY

If you have done your job well up to this point and have successfully impressed your potential customer, the sale will be automatic. The customer will walk into the store or department and buy.

TEAMWORK

When a department is redecorated, a new shop opened, or a special event in the works, are the advertising and display departments involved in what's going on? Are they as excited about it as the planners are?

It should be self-evident that a close relationship among the departments is not only advisable but essential. This is particularly true in sales promotion, which must reach out and entice the customer to the store again and again.

You will know whether this rapport exists in your store. In every store, there should be one person with the final responsibility for the presentation of the store through sales-supporting activities. To do the job properly, that person must provide the atmosphere and means for understanding and the will to cooperate. Both are steps to the cash register, and to emphasize one over the other is unwise, to say the least.

Good in theory, surely—but a problem in practice. It calls for:

Planning ahead and planning together

Adding more meetings to an already tight schedule

Free exchange of ideas (including a willingness to accept criticism and express likes and dislikes)

Once a plan is made, departments should meet to discuss implementation for total coordination

This list could probably be extended considerably, but it all boils down to a communication of ideas, a great challenge, wise use of talent, and ultimately, a better store in which to work. The display person's role in this total team will become clear as you proceed through the text.

DISPLAY DEFINED

Merchandise display is the arrangement and organization of display materials and merchandise to produce a stimulus leading to the sale of merchandise and services. It attracts the viewer's attention and induces action; it is visual selling and acts as a silent salesperson for the organization. Merchandise display is visual selling.

Good display does ten things:

1. Publicizes the business
2. Publicizes the product
3. Lays a foundation for future sales
4. Builds prestige
5. Educates the public
6. Builds up goodwill of the public
7. Offers the public useful, practical demonstrations
8. Familiarizes the public with the operations of the business
9. Supports popular trends
10. Harmonizes pure business interest with esthetics

WINDOW DISPLAY

Because the average pedestrian spends less than eleven seconds considering a window, the display has to *talk fast*. In trying to make windows do this, it may be helpful to realize that the display is an information link between the consumer and the store.

Display tells the consumer what is available, frequently at what price, and why it is desirable.

The *why* factor (*psychological motivation*) is being emphasized in sales promotion today, but it has not been used to a great extent in display. The use of psychological motivation in displays is important, because displays appeal primarily to people's emotions.

Businesses, small or large, cannot exist today by selling only replacement merchandise. They must seek the additional business derived from making merchandise emotionally or psychologically necessary. *They must create a demand for new types of consumer goods.* As an example, in recent years, men have been influenced to wear colored shirts for business. This promotion brought increased sales in shirt departments, especially in fashion-conscious areas. Oleg Cassini, noted fashion designer, agrees that visual presentation of menswear is educational, in that it dramatizes the total wardrobe and explains the value of buying the coordinated look.

The same is true of women's hosiery, sheets, towels, and almost every line of merchandise. Window displays, wherever possible, should suggest that the merchandise will give pleasure, comfort, improved appearance, or some other addition to the consumer's life.

Deodorant advertisements in national publications today emphasize the idea that using a deodorant will make a person more socially acceptable. Good window display will strive for this *benefit* technique. Every item in any store has such benefits. You have to evaluate the item in terms of how you can make it appear desirable to the consumer.

The first step in planning the window display is to consider the store's policy. The window should reflect the store's merchandising and selling policies. Most stores make use of two basic types of displays: the institutional display, which promotes the total store, its benefits, services, and image, such as a Gimbel's Christmas window; and the promotional display, which promotes one or more items of merchandise. The greater the number of merchandise items in a display, the more highly promotional the display. A detailed discussion of promotional and institutional displays follows in a later chapter. Suffice it to say that a store's total policy, whether it be promotional, semipromotional, or nonpromotional (institutional), must be reflected in its interior and exterior displays.

INTERIOR DISPLAYS

Interior displays should be designed to sell merchandise. To be effective, they must attract the eye and turn store traffic into *stoppers*—people who stop and examine the goods. The difference between a commonplace display and an outstanding one is often slight. Many times that difference consists of the right decorative touch—one that, like frosting on a cake, helps to tempt buying appetites.

Small retailers who fail to set up effective interior displays are missing opportunities for increasing their sales. According to a survey sponsored by the National Retail Merchants Association, one out of every four sales in a group of assorted independent stores occurred because of the way in which merchandise was presented in display areas.[1]

The kinds of displays used in a store depend, of course, on the types of goods handled and on the amount of space available; other considerations include budget plans and personnel to do the job.

When you present your merchandise by putting it out where people can see it, your goal is to turn store traffic into shoppers and shoppers into buyers. Whether you do it depends on the kind of display you use.

Sometimes a shopper merely looks at a display in passing. It attracts the eye but does not make a strong impression. But a good display will turn many of these lookers into stoppers who pause and study the displayed merchandise. In addition, some of the traffic that uses the store as a short cut may stop to look at an outstanding display.

Visual merchandising means the total presentation of a store and its merchandise to the customer, inside and out.

RULES FOR DISPLAY PLANNING

The following rules should be observed in planning a display:

1. Aid the eye in finding the focal point of the display easily.
2. Limit the number of competing elements in the display.
3. Give the display one dominant motif, all other ideas in the display being subordinate to it.
4. By using contrast and rhythm, add life to your colors and proportions.
5. Select display props and material having some connection with the exhibited product. Do not use display props and material that stand alone.
6. Do not allow the display props and material to take up most of the space or the best space in the window.
7. Avoid anything that conflicts or takes away from the sales message.
8. Use colors appropriate to the season.
9. Do not mix styles.

NOTES CONCERNING ALL DISPLAY PROJECTS

The text often refers to *shadow-box* areas for display practice. Shadow boxes are ideal for practicing display construction. However, if laboratory facilities do not permit the use of a number of such shadow boxes, other kinds of display areas can easily be substituted. These areas include:

Cardboard or masonite boxes of various sizes

Cases or enclosed areas in retail stores

Tabletops with pin boards of some nature behind them

[1]Gabriel M. Valenti, *Interior Display: A Way to Increase Sales,* Small Marketers Aids, No. 111 (Washington, D.C.: Small Business Administration, February 1965), p. 2.

Those students most interested in industrial display may wish to work immediately with larger areas, continuing to apply the same principles. These areas might include:

A corner of the display lab

A booth with a surface of several square feet

A bulletin board with tables in front of it

An actual company's trade-show exhibit

Along with most of the project assignments, a display packet is included that contains:

Project objectives

Project explanation

A display construction checklist

A sketch sheet

A loan sheet

An evaluation sheet

DISPLAY CONSTRUCTION CHECK LIST

1. Decide on merchandise to be displayed.   _____
2. Select display area.   _____
3. Fill in display sketch sheet.   _____
4. Lay out the showcard.   _____
5. Produce the showcard.   _____
6. Arrange to obtain merchandise (use Loan
   Sheet if necessary).   _____
7. Clean and prepare display area.   _____
8. Accumulate props.   _____
9. Put the display in the display area.   _____
10. Evaluate the display (use Evaluation Sheet).   _____
11. Return merchandise.   _____
12. Return props.   _____
13. Clean display area.   _____
14. File materials on display in project packet for use
    in final portfolio.   _____

A checklist of activities and materials to be used in display construction projects.

SUGGESTED ACTIVITIES

1. Read and make reports from such trade publications as *Visual Merchandising*. These may be written or oral reports on any aspect of display, highlighting its definition or importance.

2. Discuss the status of present-day displays and positive changes that would strengthen today's display effectiveness.
3. Seek opinions of displays in general from friends, relatives, and students from other classes. Do you find a consensus of the good and bad in displays today?

Project One: STUDENT PORTFOLIO PROJECT

Objective: To provide the student with a visible summary of his or her accomplishments in the area of lettering, sign layout, and display production. This portfolio may be used for final evaluation purposes by the instructor. The portfolio will also be used by the student when applying for employment in the field of marketing.

Assignment of the project takes place at the beginning of the semester and culminates during the last week of the semester. It is thus an ongoing, continuous activity.

The portfolio is to include the following:

1. A list of the competencies the student has mastered in the area of visual merchandising.
2. A cover that has been designed and produced by the student and that applies the principles of sign layout.
3. Three signs or showcards of varying sizes that illustrate good layout principles as well as any or all lettering styles and techniques the student has mastered.
4. A color wheel and seven color cards illustrating each of the seven color schemes discussed in the text. The color wheel is to be painted by the student from the three primary colors.
5. A photograph of each of the student's displays.
6. A written evaluation of each of the student's displays, explaining the use of each of the principles of design.
7. A description of the lighting technique used for at least three of the displays above.

The portfolio is to be evaluated on its completeness and organization.

2

Critical Elements:
the necessities

The stores of one organization we know of do more than 45 percent of their week's volume in less than twelve hours. During that time, proper merchandise display does a major portion of the selling job. Thus, the displays cut the selling time of salespeople, whom customers usually outnumber by ten to one, and the effective presentation of merchandise makes shopping easier for the customer.

Visual merchandising is studied here as an integral part of the total sales promotion process, whether it is the sale of merchandise, an image, or an idea that is the primary concern of the person or institution involved. As a student of merchandise display, you will be instructed in the *organization, planning, preparation, and arrangement of effective displays*. Included you will find the proper display methods and procedures used in the promotion and merchandising of goods and services. The methods discussed will incorporate proper display techniques and effective materials with the esthetic qualities that are in keeping with the goal of the merchant.

THE ELEMENTS OF DISPLAY

In the organization and consideration of information concerning visual merchandising, five elements may be isolated as necessary components in the production of successful display units in visually merchandised areas. These five elements of display are *merchandise, shelf or display area, props, lighting, and showcards*.

MERCHANDISE

The selection of merchandise or of an appropriate idea is the element that determines the purpose of the display and, ultimately, the final value of the display in the light of the merchandising goal. All other elements are intended to support the goal that this initial selection of merchandise or idea produces—special promotion, holiday, seasonal, high fashion, and so on. The merchandising goal, of course, is to sell the goods or services offered by the store.

SHELF OR DISPLAY AREA

Shelves and display areas provide the actual physical facility for the display. The cleaning and preparation of these areas are an integral part of the successful display. If the display area is movable, consideration should be given to appropriate placement within the total layout of the establishment.

Before the props, lighting, or showcards are considered, this physical facility must be analyzed to determine whether or not specific problems may arise involving the use of the area. During such analysis, it is important to keep in mind that the viewer's eye must move easily throughout the display, regardless of the direction from which he or she approaches.

A background increases pulling power. Often the difference between a passable display and one that makes a big impression on customers is slight. Students at New York University's Institute of Retail Management saw this fact in action when they ran a test in a suburban store.

They set up an ordinary display of three mannequins with no decorative background. The figures wore medium-priced dresses and stood on platforms in a prominent location on the selling floor. Many women passed the display without noticing it.

Then the students dressed up the display. They draped green fabric behind the mannequins and set a floral arrangement in the center of this new background. They used no special lighting. The materials for the display cost $30.

What happened when they added this small, and relatively inexpensive, imaginative touch? It was like adding frosting to a cake. An ordinary-looking display was turned into an outstanding one that shoppers began to notice, and many of them stopped to study the dresses. In fact, lookers—shoppers who turned to look as they passed—increased by more than 60 percent when the display was dressed up with the decorative background. In addition, stoppers—people who stopped and examined the dresses—increased by almost 80 percent. Interviews with customers revealed that more than 75 percent of them did not have the dress department in mind when they entered the store. They were shopping for other items or were looking around.

The display you've just read about did several things for the store. First, it showed the merchandise—dresses—to shoppers $t the place where it counted: on the selling floor. Second, it told shoppers precisely what the store was featuring, and in what styles, sizes, materials, colors, and prices. (A sign helped to convey this information.) Third, the display gave drama, excitement, and sales appeal to the medium-priced dresses. As part of a long-range program, such outstanding displays can also build a steadily growing impression on customers and prospects—impressions of quality, style, leadership, or price, for example. These programs must, however, be planned well in advance and must occur on a continuous basis for full effectiveness.[1]

PROPS

Display props include all physical objects within the display area that are not considered salable merchandise. Included are floor coverings, wall treatments, backgrounds, dummies, hems or shelves, steps, and other objects concerned with the creation of settings for the merchandise. Display props, however, must not over-shadow or dominate the salable items, or be located so that those items are hidden in

[1]Gabriel M. Valenti, *Interior Display: A Way to Increase Sales,* Small Marketers Aids, No. 111 (Washington, D.C.: Small Business Administration, February 1965), p.1.

the display, regardless of the props' uniqueness and appeal. The major purpose of display must always be kept in mind: to present aad sell merchandise to the consumer.

LIGHTING

Lighting treatments within the display are used to draw attention to either a part of the area or a specific item in the display, or to coordinate parts of the total area. These treatments may be used to emphasize items or areas; they also may be used to bring motion into the various segments of the display and to direct the viewer's eye.

Types of lights, in addition to the usual indoor lighting arrangements, include floodlights, revolving lights, black lights, colored lights, flashing lights, and spotlights.

SHOWCARDS

Showcards are a necessary part of any display. They provide the viewer with the desired information concerning salable items and their consumer benefits. They are that additional "come in" incentive so important to visual selling. Showcards are designed for appropriateness of lettering style, content, emphasis, size, and placement, so that the message they convey to the viewers will be in agreement with the purpose of the total display. (An example of one lettering procedure may be found in Chapter 16.)

Signs do the talking for a display. They give significant details about the article, such as size, styles, colors. Thus, as silent salespeople, signs answer customers' questions about price and features, and tell where the goods are located in the store. The following suggestions may be helpful in your thinking about the signs you use on your interior displays:

1. Make your signs informative. The wording should be compact and, when possible, sparkling.
2. They should look professional. Compact printing machines are available if you prefer to do your own signs.
3. See that they are not soiled or marred. Nothing spoils merchandise quicker in the customer's eyes than a soiled sign.
4. Keep signs timely by changing them often.
5. Try to make your signs sell customer benefits rather than things. Signs for clothes, for example, should sell neat appearance, style, and attractiveness rather than utility. For furniture, they should sell home life and happiness rather than just lamps and tables.[2]

FORMS TO BE USED THROUGHOUT THIS TEXT

Various forms and procedures have been adopted here to clarify the information found in this text and to expedite your understanding of it. The forms introduced here will be used throughout the text.

[2]Valenti, *Interior Display: A Way to Increase Sales,* p.3.

SKETCH SHEET

Name _____

Name _____

Name _____

Sketch # _____
                    (Display Area #)

S K E T C H

Materials from Lab: _____ (Numbers)

_____ (Numbers)

_____ (Numbers)

Outside of lab materials: _____

Merchandise: _____

Showcard theme: (Actual words to appear on card)

_____

Signature of Instructor:

_____

SKETCH SHEET FOR PLANNING THE DISPLAY

Before actual activity begins on the production of a display, the display must be planned. This planning must include the specific elements involved. Specific planning is necessary so that the display area will not be vacant while production takes place, because each moment the area is empty is lost potential for attracting customers.

This is so integral in display that it is implied from the start of one's employment. The display is completely planned, with all materials, props, and so on prepared before one display is disassembled and another constructed. Thus, in the classroom, planning is stressed and should be a part of evaluation; in reality, however, it is taken for granted as a part of the professional routine of the display artist. Constant use of this sheet will aid in creating better displays.

INVENTORY SHEET

The following list of display materials is an example of what to include in a marketing department and of what is available. Your instructor will assist you in making such a list for your specific department.

Basic necessities
   Masking tape
   White poster board
   Colored poster board
   Large stick pins
   Small common pins
   Spool thread
   Fishing line
   Thumb tacks
   Finishing nails
   Hammers
   Large scissors
   Wire cutters
   Stapler
   Staple gun
   Scotch tape
   String
   Assortment of crepe paper
   Assortment of fabrics (3-yd. pieces)
   Assortment of latex paints
   India ink
   Showcard water-color paints
   Two-sided supported screen
   Window draperies
   Circular stands
   Glass counter and case with shelf
   Open-back display window with lighting and gridded ceiling
   Closed-back display window with lighting and gridded ceiling
   Shadow boxes (either built-in or made from pegboard and plywood)[3]
   Round table
   Guidesticks
   Rulers
   Yardsticks
   Light bulbs
   Extension cords
   Ladder
   Large brooms

Large-item prop purchases (budgeted equipment for display laboratory)
   Family of mannequins
   Three turntables
   Spot- and floodlights
   Flashers for lights
   Artificial-grass carpets
   Assortment of colored carpets corresponding to window sizes
   Assortment of bricks
   Crushed cork
   Crushed styrofoam
   Bust forms
   Artificial potted plants
   T-stands

Low-budget props
   Artificial leaves
   Logs (split and whole)
   Wire garbage cans
   Construction paper
   Cardboard boxes of all sizes (can be used as shadow boxes or kiosk centers)
   Metal shelves
   Fishnet
   Pieces of plywood boards (for brick and board shelves)
   Cutawl

---

[3]Other props and materials will be constructed or refinished by the display students.

EVALUATION SHEET

After preparation, the display will be evaluated in terms of use and arrangement of merchandise and materials and of application of design principles. This evaluation will illustrate problem areas, so that each display and each person's efforts will become increasingly effective.

Table 2−1 shows a suggested evaluation procedure covering the items in display preparation that determine its effectiveness. It is to be used for both self-evaluation and an instructor's evaluation.

SUMMARY

From this point, it is possible to proceed with an orderly and comprehensive study of the art of merchandise display.

A series of demonstrations illustrating techniques of proper lighting, display-area

TABLE 2−1 Display Evaluation Sheet

Criterion	Possible Points	Points	Comments
Subject—Its appropriateness in the store situation	10		
Neatness and preparation of the display area	5		
Message and total effect	5		
Elements: Props Shelf Lighting Showcard Merchandise	10		
Organization and planning: Promptness Sketch	5		
Principles: Emphasis Harmony Balance Rhythm Proportion	10		
Color—Theme and execution	5		

preparation, and the proper arrangement of the display will be given. The topic of merchandise selection will be considered.

A series of instructional units are given involving the actual techniques of layout and lettering culminating in the production of showcards. The skills necessary for the production of these cards may actually be mastered from these.

The selection of merchandise and services deemed appropriate for displays will be discussed.

Finally, the principles of design and arrangement that will enable you to select and organize the elements of the display are presented.

SUGGESTED ACTIVITIES

1. Take a complete inventory of your display department for future reference.
2. After discussion with the instructor, decide what method of lettering will be used in your displays. Proceed with acquiring the skills and materials for future signs. (See Chapter 16.) Sufficient skills must be attained so that showcards having a professional appearance may be created for the ensuing displays.

Project Two: DISPLAY PROCESS DEMONSTRATION

Each student or small group of students will be assigned one of the following areas of information until all suggested areas are covered. These areas include:

Handling mannequins and dressing them

Pinning merchandise to a flat surface in 3-D form

Preparing shoes and hats for display

Altering the size of apparel on mannequins

Making props from paper

Lighting effects (also turntables)

Flying merchandise from overhead areas

Draping props and merchandise

Combining scarves, belts, and other small accessories

Other, optional areas

Each individual or team will visit a local merchant and observe the treatment of merchandise in the assigned area (possibly borrowing merchandise for the student's demonstration simultaneously).

A handout of the demonstration procedure will be prepared and duplicated for all members of the class, based on field research and library information.

The demonstration will be given in the class and evaluated by the instructor.

DEMONSTRATION FORMAT

Name _____

Project Team _____

Team Member _____

Instructor Evaluation _____

Class Composite Evaluation _____

Demonstration Skill(s) to Be Presented:
List and describe briefly. (For example, "To demonstrate making props from paper.")

Sketch of Demonstration Application
Components:

Materials Needed
Step-by-step explanation of the skill you are demonstrating:
1.
2.
3.

Uses of This Skill (What stores or types of displays is it used in?)

3

Origination
and
Progression

"Curtain going up. Places, everyone."

The little group moved to one side with an air of excitement. This was like opening night on their own private Broadway stage.

A tall, thin man standing against the wall looked questioningly at another man who stood just a step in front of the group. After hesitating a moment, the second man nodded, and the thin man reached up and pulled a rope. Slowly the curtains parted to open the scene to the audience.

Outside in the snow, the spectators gasped with pleasure and awe at the colorful, animated scene. Little children were lifted so that they could see over the crowd.

Inside the store, the little group of people sighed with relief. The man who had signaled the curtain raising nodded his head in satisfaction and turned away.

"Going to get some rest?" someone asked.

The man stopped. "No," he said with a smile. "I'm going to start planning next year's Christmas display."

The viewers outside started to move slowly along the windows, stopping to exclaim as they came to each new scene. Coming downtown to see the Christmas window displays at Putnam's was as much a part of preholiday activities as shopping in the store would be later on. The extra budget allowance for these magnificent scenes would more than pay for itself.

These actions and discussions take place every Christmas season, as well as on other occasions when effective, well-planned displays are created. A great deal of attention has been given to display and its artistic and profit-making function.

Where did it start? And how has display changed since then?

THE HISTORY OF DISPLAY

DISPLAY AT ITS INCEPTION

The idea of display is as old as history itself. It can be traced back to man's first inclination to decorate his body or in some other way to indulge his desire to be ostentatious and gain status in regard to his person or possessions.

However, display as we know it today was almost nonexistent until early in the twentieth century. Before then, purchasing power was limited, and there was no pressure to present the public with the full range of goods offered for sale by an establishment. Spending was mostly for staples, leaving few if any dollars for goods whose purchase might be triggered by the emotional excitement of a good display.

Later, as the economy improved, merchants tried to show their wares by cramming as many items as possible into the window display area. Or, if the store catered to the "carriage trade," the windows might contain instead, say, large oriental vases filled with artificial flowers, placed against a background of dark wood or velvet draperies. In the spring, artificial forsythia would appear in the vases, and in the fall, artificial oak leaves. By about 1922, every merchant who could afford it had gleaming backgrounds of mahogany or walnut in his windows. But still, no attempt was made to glamorize or enhance the product itself, or to place it in such a position in the window as to promote its sales appeal.

If the establishment was a large one, the constant cramming of display areas and shuffling of merchandise became an unhappy, time-consuming task in the eyes of both the merchant and the person responsible for filling and emptying the window.

DEVELOPMENT OF DISPLAY PERSONNEL

The first display person appeared on the scene to ease the problem of maintaining the crowded window area. His job was dominated by custodial overtones, and his major responsibility was to keep the merchandise clean and the window area free from debris. Merchandise was selected for the window only in terms of how much he could fit into the given space.

This person, who was known as a window trimmer, had no comprehension of artistic principles, merchandising goals, or the profit motive. His greatest expression of creativity was to occasionally place a vase of paper flowers in some vacant corner of his diffuse display of goods.

Also at this time, mannequins appeared as a display prop. They were constructed of wax and tipped the scales at about 300 pounds. Not only were they heavy and difficult to move, they often melted in the sun-heated windows, making it necessary to remove them on hot summer days. Needless to say, these original dummies left much to be desired in the way of functional display props.

DISPLAY ENTERS THE WORLD OF ART

As art forms, window and other displays may never be exhibited in our more conservative museums, but the idea that displays can be imaginative and artistic was originally conceived by artists. This idea developed in Europe soon after the end of World War I.

European artists, especially in Germany, became interested in proving that art has a functional form; that is, that good design could be used commercially. However, as display emerged from the infant to the adolescent stage, it was significantly affected by the Exposition of Decorative Arts in Paris in 1926. Those interested in the art of display for the purpose of merchandising set out to emulate in the marketplace the type of art that was exhibited at the exposition for totally esthetic purposes.

Odd and varied art objects, many of them made of plaster of paris, were constructed for display windows and had no possible use other than their questionable presence there. Merchandise was once again forgotten, this time for the sake of a new art form.

In 1938, Sigmund Freud's introduction of the concept of surrealism had an effect on the art of display. The application of psychological dream analysis to merchandising interrupted the growth of display for one mad period. Surrealism, as expressed in display windows, did stop people as they passed, but only long enough for laughter. Few display people used the theme to advantage.

However, during this period, several people gained status as professional display artists. They developed individual styles and techniques of display that have left indelible marks on the pages of display history. And the idea had developed that a window could be used to frame an artistic arrangement that would interest passersby.

Retailers gradually began to hire artists to create their window displays. Stores set up display departments and staffed them with people who were trained in art, design, and interior decoration, and who also understood merchandising. These people had the courage and the ability to develop original ideas and make use of modern art forms. Lifelike mannequins in natural poses added interest and realism to displays.

CURRENT STATUS OF DISPLAY

Today, retailers have discovered the power of attractive displays to bring people into their stores, to interest customers in their merchandise, and to create a desire for the items displayed. Through displays, especially in their store windows, they tell you what they have that is new and different and suggest ways to make you and your home more attractive. All stores, large and small, use displays to catch the attention of passersby and help sell merchandise. The best displays are designed to make you think, to appeal to your emotions, and to persuade you to buy. Table 3−1 contrasts past and present displays.

Display has now become a profession, an integral part of the promotion and sale of merchandise. Across the country today, there are many groups of resourceful and

TABLE 3−1   Past and Present Displays

Characteristics of Displays of the Distant Past	Positive Characteristics of Displays Today
Unorganized charlatanism (unprepared person practicing display)	Planned, professional, up-to-date business methods
Show window part of the storage space	Spacious display of selected merchandise
Disorderly	Systematic
Unplanned	Methodical
Poor display techniques	Artistic value
Dull and careless	Bright and careful
Bad taste	Attractive, tasteful
Negative effect	Positive effect
No selling factor	Sales promoting

imaginative men and women working against deadlines that would defeat less inventive designers. They combine artistic understanding—some, even genius—with the profit motive and pragmatism of the merchandiser. Our society looks upon them with respect and admiration, and they are amply rewarded, financially and otherwise, for their efforts. Display personnel maintain a weekly level of excellence that would be hard to equal in other fields, their windows having an esthetic cleverness that seems to reach through the glass to catch the window shopper's attention.

It is difficult to estimate the number of employees in the field. Anyone who arranges a few objects in a store window or on a counter may be considered a display person. Reliable industry sources indicate, however, that the number of professional, full-time display workers in the United States ranges between sixty and seventy thousand.

Display today is a competitive, calculating, psychoanlyzed profession of visual selling.

THE PHILOSOPHY OF DISPLAY

Display is part of our popular culture. It adds to a pleasurable environment and has a welcome usefulness as a constant, constructive stimulus to better living that promotes the products of a healthy industrial economy.

Display is a handicraft as well as an artistic occupation, designed to promote the sales and further the prestige of the business it serves. It is a specialized branch of commercial art, faced perhaps with more problems than some other branches because of the constant pressure for both creativity and performance.

Improvisation makes display fresh, spontaneous, and bright, and is the core of its vitality. Display serves its purpose briefly and then vanishes. Its creativity must run on a timetable, and much of the work's potential value is never realized, owing to the brief existence of the display and the limited audience it serves.

Display personnel constantly seek new concepts and fresh formulas. Rather than copy what has been used by others, they develop new ideas, realizing that originality must be one of their cardinal rules.

Display is art first, handicraft second. It is commercial art because it serves commerce; it is art in that it is creative, imaginative, and truly versatile. The display person must master both two- and three-dimensional techniques; use color, form, movement, lighting, and the properties of different materials to obtain the desired effects; work only for the present, although the past and the future will be featured in his or her creations; and combine the inspiration of an artist with the hands of a craftsman and the mind of a salesperson.

Some of the display person's problems lie in the duty to marry art to sales promotion and evolve these two into a harmonious entity. Sales appeal and taste must form a perfect match, free from constraint. The display person is the creator of the final, all-important phase of advertising, the one who ultimately transforms the potential customer's semiconscious interest into desire for possession, breaking down inhibiting barriers and directing the final steps toward the sales counter.

SUGGESTED ACTIVITIES

1. Make this test: Stand outside your favorite store, count the number of people stopping in front of a window, and listen to what they are saying about the display; absorb the feeling given by the audience, then draw your own conclusions and bring them back to discuss with your classmates.
2. Interview display personnel representing various types and sizes of stores in your community and attempt to determine how display has changed in the community.
3. Lettering skills, noted in the Suggested Activity in Chapter 16, may now be applied with Supplemental Practice, and students may create showcards for a specific assignment.

EVALUATION

True-False

1. The idea of display is relatively new. _____
2. Display as we know it today began around 1945. _____
3. In the first years of display, the idea of the merchant was to give the consumer an idea of the extent and line of his merchandise. _____
4. The first display person was really an artist in disguise. _____
5. The first mannequins weighed approximately 300 pounds. _____
6. Display has progressed slowly through the years. _____
7. By 1922, the least important thing in display was the background, and merchants had turned to creative presentations of good merchandise. _____
8. Display was affected significantly by the Exposition of Decorative Arts in Paris in 1926. _____
9. Windows in the 1925–1935 era became very arty in their content. _____
10. The ideas of Sigmund Freud affected display. _____
11. By the end of 1930, real professional display people began to emerge. _____
12. At the turn of the century, a great deal of walnut and mahogany was used in the background of window displays. _____
13. About 45 years ago, a lot of walnut and mahogany was used. _____
14. Display is visual selling. _____
15. Display is now a well-paid profession. _____
16. Display produces a concept of better living and promotes a healthy industrial economy. _____
17. Display adds to a pleasurable environment. _____
18. Improvisation is very bad when applied to display. _____
19. Displays have unlimited existence and unlimited audience, so display creativity is much appreciated. _____
20. Display people are essentially copyists and do not frequently seek new conceptions and fresh formulas. _____
21. Display is handicraft first and art second. _____

22. Display is commercial art. _____

23. The display person must master both two- and three-dimensional techniques. _____

24. The display person works only in the present. _____

25. The display person's problems lie in the duty to marry art with sales promotion. _____

26. Display is a two-dimensional process. _____

27. Display is the calculated application of esthetics to visual selling. _____

28. In display, merchandise possibilities must be aligned with expressive capacities. _____

29. Statistically, display defends the value of window space. _____

30. The only purpose of visual merchandising is to create a distinctive display featuring the store's merchandise. _____

31. If a store features effective, exciting displays, it is necessary to increase the number of salespeople in order to sell the merchandise to the customer. _____

32. The purpose of a display is determined only after the finishing touches are applied to it. _____

33. In the field of display, props are the mechanisms that allow mannequins to stand upright. _____

34. Lighting may be used to emphasize a particular item or area in a display. _____

35. In a merchandise display, the use of showcards is optional. _____

36. Artistic ability has never been important in the display field. _____

37. Display-department personnel of today usually have no training in merchandising or art before they are hired. _____

38. Display personnel have little status as professionals in the field of merchandising. _____

39. The duty of the display person is to combine artistry and sales promotion in his or her work. _____

Project Three: FIELDWORK

A tour may be arranged to one or more of the following places:

A display supply house

A large department store's central display department

A small store's prop room

An industrial advertising department where trade-show displays may be planned, constructed, and so on

The observations to be made on this tour include:

The preservation and care of display props

Seasonal display props

Prop ideas appealing to individual students

The construction of specific props

Procedures in utilizing props

This tour will be combined with a discussion with the head of the display department or small-store owner. Class discussion follows.

4

The Framework of Visual Merchandising

THE PRINCIPLES OF DESIGN

The principles of design are used in all art forms. When knowledgeably applied, they combine to create purposeful, effective, esthetically pleasing entities, whether in the fine arts, commercial art, or visual merchandising. In display, they appropriately coordinate all the parts of the display in varying degrees. A knowledge of these principles is imperative for the person seeking to become skilled in display. Therefore, after discussing the steps of a sale as applied in display, it seems natural to analyze a display in terms of these principles—the coordinators.

The five principles—balance, emphasis, harmony, proportion, and rhythm—will be defined and presented here briefly, and then their use and application will be more thoroughly examined in the ensuing chapters.

BALANCE

Balance may be defined artistically as *the state of equipoise between the two sides of an entity*. It involves itself with the equilibrium and weight of the different elements or opposing forces of these two sides.

Balance refers to the displaying of merchandise "in such a manner that a pleasing distribution of weight occurs. Weighing, to determine balance, involves estimating and comparing the values and importance of the two sides of the display."[1]

EMPHASIS

Emphasis simply refers to *the point that appears to be most dominant in any particular and bounded display area*. It is therefore the place at which the eye makes contact with the total display field. The several methods by which a point of eye contact or a point of emphasis may be created will be discussed in depth in the chapter dealing with emphasis.

[1]Jimmy G. Koeninger, *You Be the Judge: Display* (Columbus, O.: Ohio Distributive Education Materials Lab, 1974), p. 10.

28

HARMONY

Harmony pertains to *the agreement among the various elements of the design that are unified to obtain a pleasing effect.* Merchandise, lighting, props, shelf space, and showcards are combined through balance, emphasis, rhythm, proportion, the correct use of color, and the use of texture to create an aura of visual, artistic, and commercial agreement and correctness.

PROPORTION

Proportion is concerned with *the ratio of one aspect of the display to any other.* The relationship or ratio of merchandise to total space must be considered. One piece of merchandise must be considered in relationship to the others. The ratio of various props and showcards to the total arrangement of merchandise on display is also important. One particular object should not seem too large, too heavy, or too small in proportion to others in a display area.

RHYTHM

Rhythm involves *the measurement of motion;* motion and proportion culminate in the eventual flow that occurs in the entity.

Rhythm pertains to the path the eye takes after making initial contact with the display. It is important that the eyes of the customer are led throughout the entire display area and do not leave the display until all parts of it have been seen.

THE DISPLAY'S HOUSE—THE STORE

A store's personality is clearly shown by the way it chooses to display itself—from the bargain basement to the top floor, from the front door to the rear entrance, and all along the way. We will now discuss how the principles of design and arrangement are applied to various types of display windows in a variety of stores.

OUTSIDE THE STORE

There are all types of retailing establishments: the suburban store, the self-service store, the dealer, the exclusive shop, and so on. But whatever the type of store, its sidewalk appearance, or front, will fall into one of three general categories: arcade, straight, or angled.

The Arcade Front. Arcade fronts are usually spacious. They allow the window shopper to amble around the outside of the store, off the sidewalk, and scrutinize merchandise closely. Arcade fronts may be open in sweep or more complex, with island-type windows. They seem to be more relaxing to the shopper and often take on highly surrealistic shapes, with concave or slanted panes of glass and beautifully decorated windows. (See Figure 4−1.) Windows are the promise of the store, and they deserve careful consideration.

The Straight Front.   This type of front parallels the sidewalk, with only entrances to break its monotony. The entrances may be recessed into the main-floor area, but all the lines are identical. (See Figure 4−2.)

The Angled Front.   The angled front is much like the straight front in that it follows a true line, but the monotony is relieved by angles away from the sidewalk contour. (See Figure 4−3.)

The design of the doors or windows in an angled-front store may be asymmetri-

FIGURE 4−1 *The arcade front*

FIGURE 4−2 *The straight front*

FIGURE 4−3 *The angled front*

cal or symmetrical. Angled store fronts tend to lead the passerby toward the entrance. Often these entrances have deep lobbies to allow traffic to slow down without being pushed or pressured by other pedestrians.

DISPLAY-WINDOW TYPES

Various types of window display areas are used in planning and building a store front. They are elevated, elevator, ramped, lobby, shadow-box, corner, island or kiosk, open-back, closed-back, and semiclosed-back.

Elevated Windows.   These windows have a usual floor height of twelve to fourteen inches above the sidewalk level. This is mostly a safety measure, to protect the expensive glass panes from damage by shuffling feet, cleanup crews, and vibration caused by passing vehicles. A floor of this height also helps get the displayed merchandise closer to eye level, where it can be seen more easily. Some stores have elevated windows with floors 24 to 36 inches above the sidewalk to accommodate the type of merchandise sold. Jewelry stores, bookshops, optical stores, and bakeries fall into this category. (See Figure 4−4.)

Elevator Windows.   These are the display person's dream. They are desirable because their floor level may be raised or lowered at will; but they are very expensive to install, since they require a complicated hydraulic system. With this type of window setup, display departments are usually located in the basement; for changing the display, the window is lowered one floor, trimmed, and then raised to the desired elevation.

Ramped Windows.   These are actually only a variation of a standard window. The main difference is that their floors are slanted, elevated in the back to form a ramp-like display area. Such windows facilitate showing merchandise attached to a panel. Any

FIGURE 4—4 *Elevated windows*

window may be made a ramp window merely by installing a false floor with its back edge higher than the front. Many bakeries, banks, utility buildings, shoe shops, and drugstores employ this type of window for their displays.

Lobby Windows.   Just as its name implies, this kind of display area follows the lines of deeply recessed entrances to buildings. Lobby windows are usually slightly angled to help lead the customer right into the store. They present a display problem because people must be attracted coming and going as well as straight on.

Shadow-box Windows.   These may be small and an entity in themselves, or they may be segments of a larger window that has lost space to a structural block. Grillwork, unsightly pipes, posts, and doorways are camouflaged very nicely in frontage layouts by the placement of shadow-box windows. They also afford a display area for small merchandise such as jewelry, toys, cosmetics, notions, books, handkerchiefs, infant shoes, and so on.

Corner Windows.   These are often considered the most important areas of any store frontage. They are the central viewing point of converging traffic, and consequently, the best merchandising areas. The average pedestrian will notice a corner window and its contents much more readily than a side-street window.

Island or Kiosk Windows.   These are usually found in arcade fronts and are isolated from the rest of the building. This type of window offers many display problems because it can be seen from all angles, and merchandise must be placed so as to appear attractive from all sides.

Open-back Windows.   Since the end of World War II, there has been a trend, both in remodeling and in new building, toward opening the store to full view of the sidewalk traffic. Thus far, the trend has mostly been confined to the small stores, and whether there is to be a definite swing toward open-backed windows remains to be seen.

Many retailers have found that this type of window stimulates. It invites the passerby to come in and look around. Properly handled, open-back windows become quite effective. Replacing the lost stock and storage areas and maintaining effective displays without blocking a clear view of the store are but two of the problems that arise here and require added ingenuity on the part of the display person.

Semiclosed-back Windows.   These windows, having a partition extending to a height below the line of vision, are sometimes found in drugstores and hardware stores. They offer a display challenge because they must be constructed giving consideration to the store interior.

Closed-back Windows.   These windows completely isolate the display area from the store; they are found in the majority of department stores and in specialty stores handling men's and women's wearing apparel. A display may be constructed in them without the additional considerations of lighting and merchandise arrangement within the store.

Stores with off-the-street parking lots are giving less attention to display windows along their forntage, because their shoppers park in the first vacant space and seek the nearest entrance. Many stores overcome this inability to influence with window displays by placing huge display areas directly inside the entrances or wherever there is heavy traffic, such as near elevators or escalators.

An innovation of city beautification committees is the shopping-center mall. These core areas, often with partially covered walkways, have fountains, benches, and meandering courts as well as broad, terrazzo-edged, landscaped malls. Here the displays and windows are most influential upon the passerby in the selection of a store to patronize.

INSIDE THE STORE

All furnishings of the store should be placed to enhance the visual impression each floor presents. They should be arranged both to sell the most merchandise and to be pleasing to the customer.

Corner Shops.   These shops, as well as other marked-off areas with a distinctive decor, are sometimes employed by store engineers to relieve the monotony of departmental furnishings.

Shelves.   Obviously, shelves are necessary to store stocked merchandise. They are poor display areas, however, and should be hidden whenever possible by walls, curtains, and so on.

Counter and Table Displays.   These sell merchandise more readily than shelf displays do, because they are located in front of the stock areas, bringing the goods nearer to the customer and allowing the customer to feel and touch the merchandise. Square and rectangular shapes are the usual design for counters and cases. However, rounded, oval, and surrealistically shaped counters not only ease the flow of traffic through a store; they appear less regimented and do not present hazardous sharp edges to the customer. They are a pleasant change from the squareness of design that the shelves present.

An arrangement device that will increase sales at no added expense to the store owner is the placement of store furnishings at an angle to the structural lines of the interior. If all aisles are straight from front to back, the customer moves too quickly through the store. Even a slight deviation from the usual parallel placement will lead people in a more comfortable and leisurely path, slowing them down and inviting them to take notice of the surroundings. Likewise, when customers are leaving, counters carefully arranged at angles to the wall will seem to hold them back, to delay their departure. Each hesitation on the part of the passerby is an opportunity for interior displays to make a sale.

Shadow Boxes.   A shadow-box display is often located behind the counter area. This location makes it easy to display and maintain an arrangement of merchandise that is beyond the reach of anyone who might otherwise remove it from the store without paying for it. A more dramatic presentation of merchandise is required, however, in order to compensate for the customer's inability to handle and examine the goods. What a customer could not comprehend except by touching the merchandise must now be shown vividly.

Shadow-boxes are larger than their name would imply; in many instances, they are enclosed with glass, and they are often cleverly designed. Shadow boxes are illuminated with side, ceiling, or indirect lighting of greater intensity than their surrounding areas, so that they will attract attention immediately.

Ledges.   The tops of shelves sometimes serve as areas for display. They necessarily follow the set structural lines of a department. Ledge areas may be made very attractive with the addition of decorative pieces for seasonal promotions. Because ledges with shelf space under them are above the comfortable range of vision, constant care must be exercised in the placement of merchandise. Unsightly portions of it, such as chair seats, shoe soles, wrong sides of materials, or unfinished backs of stoves or refrigerators, should not be visible to the customer's eye and must be camouflaged with decorative effects.

Kiosks or Island Areas.   As their name implies, these are isolated display places amid the pattern of shelves and counters that constitute the principal selling spaces of a store. They are forceful merchandising agents when placed strategically near elevators, by entrances to departments, and at stairway landings. Island displays catch the customer's fancy and attract the eye. They are not stock areas, nor should they be crowded with boxes and signs. They are concerned exclusively with showing merchandise and items related to that merchandise.

Kiosks may be built from five to twenty-eight inches above the floor, may or may not have a background, and are often finished with carpet, grass, linoleum, or wood. They are well illuminated and allow space for figures, forms, and other fixtures necessary to the merchandise.

All store furnishings, of whatever description, should complement the impression desired for a certain section of a store. Plush-covered poufs would be out of place in a toy or camp-equipment department. Glass shelves are much more practical for jewelry or handbags than they are for heavy cans of paint. Island display areas are desirable for children's apparel departments, but sectional room displays are far more useful in furniture departments. As the needs of a department change, the store furnishing should be converted to meet these needs whether they are sectional or seasonal.

The importance of store furnishings cannot be overemphasized in regard to the impression a store and its wares make upon the public. Furnishings lead the customer through all departments; they provide the clerk with areas for stocking, showing, and selling merchandise; they serve as feature display areas to attract the customer. Furnishings—their type and placement—play a leading role in the dramatic presentation of merchandise.

SUMMARY

Display has been analyzed several ways in this chapter. In review, let us look at these different views or approaches to display study:

1. Steps of sale through display
   a. Attract attention
   b. Arouse interest
   c. Create desire
   d. Win confidence
   e. Cause decision
2. Preview of display principles of design and arrangement
   a. Balance
   b. Emphasis
   c. Harmony
   d. Proportion
   e. Rhythm
3. The store
   a. Types of store fronts
   b. Types of windows
   c. Shelves and counters

SUGGESTED ACTIVITIES

1. Evaluate some downtown or suburban shopping-center windows, using the five steps of the sale through display. Determine if the displays you observe entice you to buy (or want to buy) the merchandise. If possible, evaluate the same windows that your classmates do, so that the evaluated windows can be discussed by most of the class, thereby providing a deeper understanding of the steps of the sale through display.

2. Select a two- or three-block section of the business district and note the various types of store fronts used. Attempt to interview the manager or display person of these businesses on why particular fronts were used.

Project Four: PROP CONSTRUCTION, ACCUMULATION, AND REFINISHING

This project has several intents:

To furnish the student with at least two props to be used in one of the several displays that he or she will be completing during the semester.

To provide the student with knowledge concerning the construction of props and the ease with which simple, available items may be utilized in the displaying of merchandise.

To provide the display laboratory with a fresh supply of varied props for use during the semester.

I. Making a prop:
   A. Each student will decide what type of prop to construct and what material it will need.
   B. The prop will then be identified as appropriate for use in one of the display areas to be assigned in the future (a shadow-box prop, a kiosk prop, and so on). Planning for future course activities thus begins to take place.
   C. The selected props are to be approved and later evaluated by the instructor.
II. Refinishing, or otherwise acquiring, a prop:
   A. Each student will determine whether to visit a local business or industry and obtain a display prop that the company will donate or lend, or whether to obtain, from any number of sources, a prop that needs refinishing (painting, antiquing, rebuilding, and so on).
   B. The prop will then be identified as appropriate for use in another of the display areas to be treated in future assignments.
   C. The selected display prop and the area for which it has been identified are to be approved by the instructor.
III. The props of each student will be presented, to acquaint the class with the laboratory's total facilities and furnish an explanation of the virtues and flexibility of the prop.

5

The Design Principles of Balance and Emphasis

BALANCE

Balance is a state of equilibrium—the equality of two things in weight, force, and quantity. To balance is to compare as to relative importance, value, and weight.

In this field of merchandise display, balance is the drawing of an imaginary line down the center of a display to get two equal sides of a display area's shapes, colors, and object placement.

The following are ways in which display components might be different, but in balance:

Use exact objects in both parts of the display.

Use in the two parts of the display different-sized objects that, by their placement, will appear in balance. For example, a small item placed in the foreground will balance a larger item placed in the background. See Figure 5–1.

Balance objects of a brighter hue (color) with larger objects that have less intensity of color.

Balance smaller objects with larger objects by the frequency with which they appear. For example, one large item can be balanced with two or more smaller items. See Figure 5–2.

TYPES OF BALANCE

Generally speaking, there are two types of balance, formal and informal. Formal balance occurs when each object on the right side has an exact counterpart on the left side relative to size, placement, shape, and color. Therefore, each side has equal power to attract attention and is equally forceful in demanding the customer's action. Formal balance produces a feeling by the total unit of dignity, restraint, and conservatism. This type of balance is usually used to depict tradition, store image (or other institutional examples), and so on, and denotes less activity than the informal type.

Informal balance in display also achieves component equality to the viewer's eye, but it does so by using varieties of color, placement, size, and shape of the objects on opposite sides of the display. Using this type of balance to create a display can result in more subtle and imaginative arrangements. It is used in merchandising when the designer wishes to provide activity, excitement, and variety.

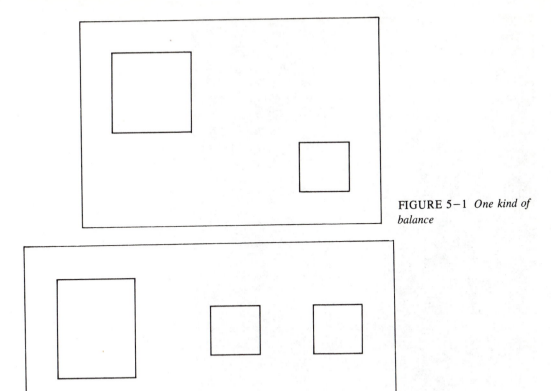

FIGURE 5–1 *One kind of balance*

FIGURE 5–2 *Another kind of balance*

DETERMINATION OF BALANCE

To determine balance in any display, do this:

1. Draw an imaginary line down the center of the display.
   a. To achieve formal balance, place objects, weight for weight, on either side of the line.
   b. To achieve informal balance, place merchandise and props so that more weight occurs on one side than on the other. Usually the side weighing the most will be on the left side, since the upper right side is the end of the eyes' path and often has little merchandise in it.
2. Place heavier objects and stronger colors closer to the floor or base of the display to avoid top-heaviness.

BALANCE AND SYMMETRY IN DISPLAY

A symmetrically balanced composition must consist of a dominant centerpiece and subsidiary motifs forming the flanks, suitably reduced in size. Motifs consist of "themes" or subjects to be elaborated on and developed. Any prominent lettering,

FIGURE 5-3 *An example of informal display*
Courtesy of Gimbels Midwest, Inc., Milwaukee, Wis.

such as signs or banners, should also be symmetrically distributed in a formal display. Smaller items such as small showcards can well be placed asymmetrically without disturbing effects. The need for symmetry is greatest when a large number of different articles are to be displayed in one composition. It is also quite often used when displaying exclusive, expensive merchandise, as when only one item (such as a designer dress) is used in a display. Symmetry implies strict correspondence in the form, size, arrangement, and so on, of parts on either side of that median line referred to above.

In asymmetrically arranged (informal) displays, one side is more dominant than the other, and the areas on either side of an imaginary line down the middle do not "weigh" the same. Asymmetrical displays lend themselves to a great deal of originality and are frequently considered to be more "creative" than the symmetrical or formal display.

FIGURE 5-4 *Smaller objects with a brighter hue (color) will balance with larger objects that have less intensity of color*

Courtesy of Gimbels Midwest, Inc., Milwaukee, Wis.

FIGURE 5–5 *An actual example of formal balance in display*
Courtesy of Chas. A. Stevens & Co., Inc.

When planning a display area, the first thing a display person determines is usually whether to balance it formally or informally. This planning can be done on paper rather than by trial and error in the display area itself. Effective balance is so important that without it, display would not usually be functional.

EMPHASIS

Webster's Dictionary defines *emphasis* as, "A forcefulness of expression that gives special impressiveness, calls to special attention . . . ; stress . . . given to a certain part or feature . . . ."

In a merchandise display, *emphasis is the point of initial eye contact*. It is from this point that all other eye movements emanate and flow; therefore, it is the center of attraction. It begins the flow of the eye throughout the entire display area that contains the merchandise.

PLACEMENT OF THE POINT OF EMPHASIS

The point of emphasis may be appropriately placed in one of two positions as the viewer faces the display.

It may occur in or very near the optical center of the display. This is halfway

FIGURE 5–6 *An actual example of informal display. Main floor Christmas post trim with a Victorian feeling*

from either side and slightly above the bottom half. With this type of emphasis placement, the eye will flow evenly on all sides of the point of emphasis, eventually covering the entire area.

The point of emphasis may also be placed in the upper left corner of the display area as it is viewed from the front. This type of placement assumes that the eye of the viewer will proceed like that of a person reading a page—from upper left to lower right—thereby covering the entire display area.

When a display is approached from either side rather than from front and center, it is advisable to place a secondary emphasis point on each wing of the area. The passerby will then be halted visually, pausing so that the primary point of emphasis will come into view, and the eye will, once again, proceed throughout the entire display.

METHODS OF CREATING EMPHASIS POINTS

The display director must keep in mind that the eye must have a point of beginning and that this point has to be planned and created.

A point of emphasis may occur through use of one of the following devices:

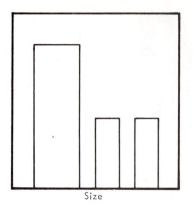

Size

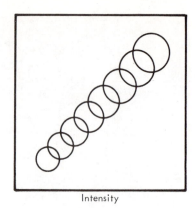

Intensity

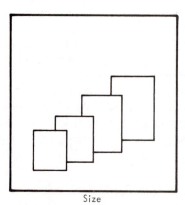

Optical Center

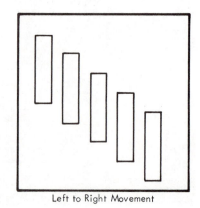

Left to Right Movement

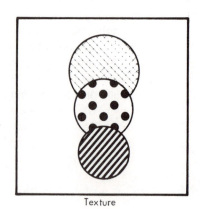

Size

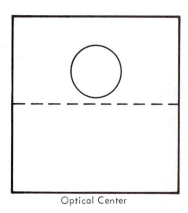

Texture

FIGURE 5–7 *Emphasis*

44

A contrast of a visually projecting color, such as a red dot on a neutral background.

A contrasting shape, such as a circular object in a field of horizontal and vertical lines.

A contrasting texture, such as a velvet object on a smooth and dull surface, or a highly reflective metallic item on a background of nonreflective woods.

A particularly large object that, although it is in proportion to the total field, is clearly dominant in terms of its importance in the display area.

See Figure 5—3 for some examples.

SUGGESTED ACTIVITIES

1. Evaluate, in terms of balance and emphasis, downtown business windows with your classmates and report on your findings to the class.
2. Find magazine articles (as recent as possible) pertaining to the use of emphasis and formal and informal balance in display.
3. Contact display equipment companies and obtain literature pertinent to this unit. Report on it.
4. Make sketches applying to the principles of design and arrangement that were explained in this chapter.

Project Five: PREPARATION AND PRESENTATION OF DISPLAY SLIDES

Procedure:

1. Select an area in which to photograph a minimum of ten displays. These areas may be suburban shopping centers, urban retail areas, nests of boutiques, or industrial trade shows.
2. Visit the area selected and photograph ten different displays in a variety of display facilities, including as many different types of counters, kiosks, windows, and shelf areas as possible.
3. Then script the slides for presentation in class. This script will include an analysis of each display according to the elements of display and the principles of design and arrangement, thus giving the student a review of both areas.
4. The slides and script will be presented to the class and evaluated by the instructor.
5. The slides and script will be submitted to the display instructor and will remain in the department, and/or will become part of the student's display portfolio, explained in Project One.

6

The Design Principles of Harmony, Proportion, and Rhythm

FIVE ASPECTS OF HARMONY

As we discussed in Chapter 4, harmony has to do with the agreement among the elements of a display. The elements we refer to are, of course, merchandise, lighting, props, shelf space, and showcards.

Let us now inspect harmony in display in terms of its application to effective production.

Harmony may be achieved through use of the artistic devices of line, shape, size, texture, and idea. Each of these devices will be discussed in terms of definition and application.

LINE

There are four basic types of lines to be used in design creation (see Figure 6−1).

Vertical Lines. The vertical line is a line whose direction is from the top to the bottom of a given area. This is a straight, upright line and gives a rigid, severe, and masculine quality to an area. *It expresses strength and stability and is inherent in many types of merchandise constructed of rigid materials.* Its application naturally gives the viewer an up-and-down eye movement.

Vertical lines may appear in the center of a display, to either side, or throughout the area in varying degrees to achieve an effect. Not all vertical lines need extend all the way from the bottom to the top of the area; they may terminate at any point in between. The points at which vertical lines terminate lend aspects of height and proportion to a display.

Dominant use of vertical lines in a display tends to heighten the area, giving the illusion of increased space in this direction.

Horizontal Lines. Horizontal lines extend across the surface of an area from one side to the other, terminating at any point in between. *They tend to widen the surface on which they are used and seemingly decrease the height of the area.*

Horizontal lines create a feeling of rest, relaxation, and repose, as in the restful line of the horizon. Merchandise that connotes rest and relaxation by its nature and use may be aptly displayed through the use of horizontal lines. These lines may be created by props or by the merchandise itself.

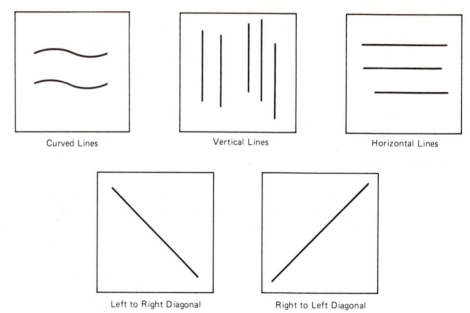

Curved Lines   Vertical Lines   Horizontal Lines

Left to Right Diagonal   Right to Left Diagonal

FIGURE 6–1 *Line harmony*

Although horizontal and vertical lines may both appear in a display area, a feeling of either the vertical or horizontal is usually dominant.

Diagonal Lines. Diagonal lines direct the eye in one of two ways. They may extend from the upper left to the lower right side of a display, thus creating and inducing action. The eye will follow this line direction with active force. This type of diagonal line especially connotes action and movement to the viewer and is quite effective in the informal display arrangement.

The diagonal line that moves from upper right to lower left is used less frequently. It tends to give the illusion of instability. It must be used with care and precision and by an expert.

Curved Lines. Curved lines add flowing movement and excellent eye direction to a display. They also tend to give a display a feminine atmosphere.

When any of the four types of lines are repeated throughout a display area, they emphasize themselves and create the simplest kind of harmony. Used in opposition to one another, they can create contrast and visual transitions. (Technically, any line that cuts across from one opposing line to another is transitional.) These transitional lines lead easily from one line to another, thus leading the eye throughout the display if used correctly. If too many lines oppose each other and the eye is asked to make a large number of transitions within a limited space, confusion results. Therefore, opposing lines should be used carefully and with expertise. Line harmony is the most important aspect of harmony in display, especially in background treatments and the control of eye movement.

SHAPE

The shape of an object refers to the visual form of that object. For our purpose, shapes are discussed not in their variations, but as being similar or dissimilar. For the creation of perfect harmony in a display, shapes that correspond exactly to one another are used exclusively.

Inharmonious or dissimilar shapes may be used in a display to create contrast and, in some instances, a point of emphasis.

SIZE

Size refers to the physical magnitude, extent, bulk, and dimension of something. To achieve harmony within a display, sizes should be kept consistent. Objects of the sizes in which they appear in reality should constitute an entire area, rather than being used in conjunction with objects that are miniatures.

Sizes should also be kept in proportion, so that large objects do not minimize smaller ones that appear with them in a display.

TEXTURE

Texture is the aspect of harmony that relates to the sense of touch. This sense may be stimulated either physically or visually, as when one senses the roughness of sandpaper without feeling it or the softness of satin without handling it.

Textures may be divided into two categories: (1) *those materials that appear rough or smooth to the touch,* and (2) *those textures that reflect light as opposed to those that absorb light.*

When a majority of the textures in a display area tend to be either smooth, rough, reflective, or absorbent, we may consider the display to have consistency and harmony.

When a combination of visual impressions prevails, the display will have contrast. If all textures are of one type with the exception of one item of a different texture, a point of contrast, or emphasis, has been created.

IDEA

In the area of merchandise display, one of the basic rules is to allow one idea to dominate. This tends to enhance the selling message of the window. Here, more than in other areas of design, we emphasize the importance of the display area as a selling tool. A display is not an artistic creation stimulating speculation and interpretation concerning its intent. The idea of a window must be clearly and quickly received by the viewer. Its details must be in keeping with the central idea or theme in order to enhance and immediately clarify the idea that prevails.

GUIDELINES IN CREATING HARMONY

The effective use of the aspects of harmony given above will produce a display that is concise in its message and pleasing to the eye of the all-important customer. In addition, keep in mind these guidelines:

1. Avoid overcrowding the space with too many shapes, whether they occur in lines, surfaces, or bodies.
2. Remember that the window or display area has to hold the merchandise and present a sales message.
3. Converging lines (lines that come together) and diverging lines (lines that seem to separate) are an aid in producing the illusion of depth through the use of perspective.
4. The curved line can be effectively combined with the various types of straight lines.
5. Give all components equal optical weight or allow one component to dominate over the others. For example, combine several vertical lines compactly with fine horizontal lines.

ELEMENTS OF PROPORTION

As you will recall from an earlier chapter, proportion refers to the ratio of merchandise to the total display area and the effective handling of the space intervals between objects. These space intervals govern the appearance of a display.

There are four commonly used space divisions or types of arrangements by which the display person achieves proportion: (1) *pyramid*, (2) *step*, (3) *zigzag*, and (4) *repetition*. (See Figure 6–2.)

PYRAMID

The pyramid is a triangular arrangement with a broad base rising to a center peak. It is a common device to achieve proportion and may be used with any type of merchandise. It tends to give a display a stiff and formal feeling.

STEP

The step is a level elevation within the display area. It is effectively used as a side unit facing the center of attraction. It is more informal than the pyramid and is most effective when only three hems or steps are used. When steps extend evenly from either side to a midpoint within the display, the appearance is of an inverted pyramid. This aspect of proportion may therefore be easily combined with the illusion of the pyramid.

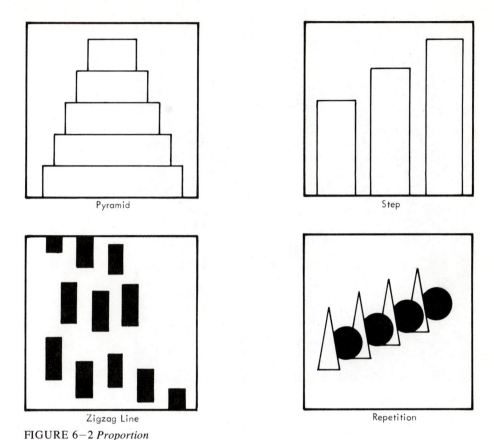

FIGURE 6–2 *Proportion*

ZIGZAG

The zigzag is based on the principle of the double reverse curve and is particularly adaptable to wearing apparel, owing to the flexibility and ease of draping most fabrics. The zigzag requires equidistant spacing and precision. It may be especially effective when small accessory hems or steps are used, thereby eliminating vacant areas. An easily achieved zigzag effect is created by using material like yarn, rope, or ribbon to lead the eye throughout the zigzag line.

REPETITION

Repetition, as a type of proportion, is simple in form. It makes use of steps of the same general nature. *It aligns all items in the same manner by height, spacing, and the angle at which they are placed.* This type of repetitive arrangement requires deviations to break the monotonous effect that may evolve.

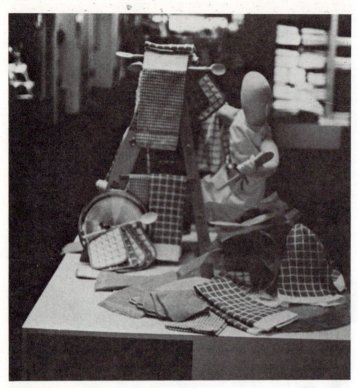

FIGURE 6—3 *Pyramid type of arrangement*
Courtesy of Gimbels Midwest, Inc., Milwaukee, Wis.

RHYTHM AND ITS ASPECTS

Rhythm is concerned with the devices employed in merchandise display that guide the eye from its point of contact throughout the remainder of the display area. Whether the viewer's eye comes in contact with the merchandise on display is contingent upon how successfully the following aspects of rhythm are applied. Any one of these four aspects will successfully guide eye movement in the desired direction. (See Figure 6—4.)

REPETITION OF SHAPES

This self-explanatory principle makes use of *similar shapes at regular intervals throughout the display.* Separate units within the display should not be apparent when this technique is employed.

Repetition of Shape

Progression of sizes

Continuous Line Movement

Radiation

FIGURE 6–4 *Rhythm*

PROGRESSION OF SIZES

Progression of sizes refers to using similar shapes and varying their sizes by consistently increasing or decreasing them along the visual path. The eye is made to move rapidly over the display, and this swift eye movement is in keeping with the immediate, quick viewing that is essential to successful displaying of merchandise.

CONTINUOUS LINE MOVEMENT

This aspect of rhythm makes wide use of curves in their varying forms. One curved line is seen leading into the next, creating a graceful, swinging movement easily followed by the onlooker's eye. Such props as ribbon lend easy eye movement by connecting curved lines. Background draping and merchandise that is easily draped can be successfully employed in achieving the effect of continuous line movement.

RADIATION

Radiation can be described as having a sunburst effect. It often appears as an inherent part of the merchandise, as in the spokes that radiate from the center of a wheel. The movement of radiation grows out of a central point and is most effectively placed at the optical center of the display. The movement may lead the eye away from the central point of contact, or it may bound the eye movement by employing an outer encircling band.

SUGGESTED ACTIVITIES

1. Photograph several current displays in the area. Then, with the assistance of the audio-visual department or your instructor, construct a combination slide/overhead presentation so that the displays (by drawing on the projection through the use of the overhead) may be visually analyzed in terms of the principles of design and arrangement.
2. Discuss how the following exist in the home, school, place of work, and local newspaper, and their effect on us:

   Five aspects of harmony

   Elements of proportion

   Rhythm

3. Present a written and oral demonstration, twenty minutes in length, on one aspect of harmony and how it affects our lives.

EVALUATION

1. List the elements of a display.
2. List the principles of design.
3. List the four aspects of rhythm.
4. List the four aspects of proportion.
5. What are the two types of balance?
6. List the five aspects of harmony.

Completion

1. _____ is particularly concerned with the path the eye takes after having made contact with a particular bounded area and the completeness with which this path proceeds throughout the whole.
2. _____ may be defined as the agreement between the many parts and aspects of any entity.
3. _____ is the equality of ratios, or a relation among quantities.
4. _____ may be artistically defined as the state of equipoise between the totals of the two sides of an entity.

5. _____ is the point that appears to be predominant in any particular bounded display area.

True-False

1. The principles of design do not pervade all art forms. _____
2. A knowledge of design principles is imperative for the person seeking to become adept in the display field. _____
3. "A forcefulness of expression that gives special impressiveness" is Webster's definition of *emphasis*. _____
4. Proportion is the equality of two things in weight, force, and quantity. _____
5. Balance is determined by drawing an imaginary line down the center of the display area. _____
6. There are two types of balance. _____
7. Used in display, formal balance is that type of balance that achieves component equality. _____
8. Informal display is used in merchandising when the designer wishes to provide activity, excitement, and variety in the creation. _____
9. At its best, symmetry should contain the eye movement within the display. _____
10. The eye should never be allowed to leave the display. _____
11. An asymmetrically balanced composition must consist of a dominant centerpiece and subsidiary motifs forming the flanks. _____
12. The need for symmetry is greatest when a large number of different articles are displayed in one composition. _____
13. Top-heaviness in a display can be avoided by placing the heavier objects and colors closer to the floor. _____
14. Emphasis is the point of initial eye contact in any given merchandise display grouping. _____
15. The point of emphasis is, therefore, the center of attraction in a display. _____
16. A point of emphasis may be placed for effective eye movement in the upper right corner of the display area as it is viewed from the front. _____
17. The eye does not always need a point of beginning. _____
18. There are four basic types of lines to be used in design creation. _____
19. The vertical line is a line whose direction is from the top to the bottom of a given area. _____
20. The diagonal line expresses strength and stability and is inherent in many types of merchandise constructed of rigid materials. _____
21. The points at which vertical lines terminate lend aspects of height and proportion to a display. _____
22. Horizontal lines tend to lengthen the surface on which they are used and seemingly decrease the height of the area. _____
23. The diagonal line that moves from right to left is used less frequently and tends to give the illusion of instability. _____
24. Curved lines are feminine for the most part. _____
25. Line harmony is the least important aspect of harmony. _____

26. Inharmonious or dissimilar shapes may be used in a display.   _____
27. Sizes should be kept in proportion to one another.   _____
28. Texture is the aspect of rhythm that relates to the sense of touch.   _____
29. The idea of a window must be clearly and quickly received by the viewer.   _____
30. Converging and diverging lines are an aid to producing the illusion of depth through the use of perspective.   _____
31. In all these combinations, the simplest and soundest principle of all is to use as many definite lines as possible in a display.   _____
32. The pyramid is a triangular arrangement with a broad base rising to a center peak.   _____
33. The step that is a level elevation within the display area is effectively used as a side unit facing the center of attraction.   _____
34. The zigzag is based on the principle of the double reverse curve.   _____
35. Whether or not the viewer's eye comes in contact with the merchandise on display is contingent upon how successfully the aspects of rhythm are applied.   _____
36. By use of the principle of similar shapes and varying their sizes by consistently increasing or decreasing them along the visual path of the view, the eye is made to move very slowly over the display.   _____
37. Repetition of shapes makes wide use of curves in their varying forms.   _____
38. Props such as ribbon lend easy eye movement in a display.   _____
39. Radiation can be described as having a sunburst effect.   _____
40. The movement of radiation grows out of a center point.   _____
41. It is usually not necessary to go through all five steps of a sale in order to sell merchandise to a customer.   _____
42. It is impossible for a display to "sell" merchandise to a customer.   _____
43. Elevated display windows are found in many types of stores, such as bakeries, jewelry stores, and bookshops.   _____
44. After a pleasing floor arrangement has been established in a store, it should never be changed.   _____
45. The most desirable arrangement of store furnishings is the placement of counters and tables parallel to the interior walls.   _____
46. Glass shelves are more appropriate for the display of jewelry or handbags than for the display of hardware.   _____
47. Rhythm in a display is determined by drawing an imaginary line down through the center of the display.   _____
48. Effective displays can be created by combining regular merchandise with a few miniatures of the same type. This creates interest in the display.   _____
49. Window displays should be planned so as to allow the eye of the passerby to flow in a leisurely manner throughout the display area.   _____

Project Six: CONSTRUCTION OF OPEN SHADOW-BOX DISPLAYS

The purpose of this project is to give experience in combining the elements of display through the use of design principles by the construction of a small, five-sided, complete display. It is an individual effort in applying knowledge of display.

Each student will construct a display using merchandise and props approved by the instructor. The display may be constructed in any five-sided area that is, optimally, visible only from the front. A sketch of the display plan should be presented to the instructor (see sketch sheet that follows).

Merchandise is to be selected and furnished by the student for the shadow box. It may be obtained through borrowing from a retail store or may be brought from the student's home. The unit value of the merchandise should be kept in mind when determining the amount of merchandise to use. The less expensive the merchandise, the more items of it need to appear in the display area to make it economically feasible.

The display area may be lighted from above or from the front.

A showcard must be constructed that fits the theme of the display, helps to provide information, and strengthens the sales message of the display.

When the elements of the display are successfully combined through use of the principles of design, the student should view the display from directly in front of the display area, then from both the left and the right sides by passing in front of it approximately three feet away, as a pedestrian or store customer would.

If, at this point, the display meets the satisfaction of the student, he or she is ready for oral and written evaluation by the instructor.

Each shadow-box display should take from one to one and a half hours to construct and from six to ten minutes to be evaluated.

After the display is evaluated, it is disassembled, the props are returned to the prop room (or to private donors), and the merchandise is carefully inspected and returned to its source. The display shelf should be cleaned and prepared for use by another student.

DISPLAY CONSTRUCTION CHECK LIST

1. Decide on merchandise to be displayed. _____
2. Select display area. _____
3. Fill in display sketch sheet. _____
4. Lay out the showcard. _____
5. Produce the showcard. _____
6. Arrange to obtain merchandise (use Loan Sheet if necessary). _____
7. Clean and prepare display area. _____
8. Accumulate props. _____
9. Put the display in the display area. _____
10. Evaluate the display (use Evaluation Sheet). _____
11. Return merchandise. _____
12. Return props. _____
13. Clean display area. _____
14. File materials on display in project packet for use in final portfolio. _____

SKETCH SHEET

Name _____

Name _____

Name _____

Sketch # _____

(Display Area #)

S K E T C H

Materials from Lab: _____ (Numbers)

_____ (Numbers)

_____ (Numbers)

Outside of lab materials: _____

Merchandise: _____

Showcard theme: (Actual words to appear on card)

_____

Signature of Instructor:

_____

Group # _____

Area _____

Name _____

Grade _____

DISPLAY EVALUATION SHEET

Criteria	Possible Points	Points	Comments
Subject—Its appropriateness in the store situation	10		
Neatness and preparation of the display area	5		
Message and total effect	5		
Elements: Props Shelf Lighting Showcard Merchandise	10		
Organization and planning: Promptness Sketch	5		
Principles: Emphasis Harmony Balance Rhythm Proportion	10		
Color—Theme and execution	5		

7

Color:

the life of a display

A window display is seen as a flashing picture by the average pedestrian, who approaches it, observes it, and responds to it, all in less than eleven seconds. This picture must be magnetic in order to bring customers into the store. A window display should represent the store and it should help sell goods. To do this, it must attract the eye and turn walkers into *stoppers*—people who stop to examine the goods.

One of the strongest forces in stopping the pedestrian and making him or her want an item is the effective use in a display of *color*. Color is one of the most important factors in creating a display. It is an invaluable selling tool, because people are color-conscious. Newspapers, magazines, radio, and television promote color constantly. Color helps to create interest in new merchandise and the desire for it.

COLOR DEFINED

We define color here as in its simplest state, rather than in the complex chemical and physical state in which it exists. Color, as we understand it, is basically *the presence or absence of light as it is reflected or not reflected from a surface.* Those that we see as light colors—yellow, say, or orange—reflect a great deal of light, and an object that reflects light completely appears to be white. Objects that absorb a great deal of light appear to have dark colors, such as purple, and complete absorption of light on a surface makes that surface appear to be black.

Colors are wavelengths of light. At one end of the spectrum of radiant energy are radio waves and infrared waves (waves of heat that are very long and invisible). At the opposite end of the spectrum are the invisible, very short, ultraviolet waves, followed by even shorter cosmic-ray waves. Between the very long and invisible sound and infrared waves at one end of the spectrum and the very short and invisible ultraviolet and cosmic waves at the other end are the waves of radiant energy that are visible. These waves are the components of visible light that we call *color*.

COLOR SYSTEMS

When describing a color, we refer to its *hue* (color and hue will be used here interchangeably), to its *chroma* or *intensity,* and to its *value. Hue* is the name of the color: red, yellow, blue, and so on. *Chroma,* or *intensity,* is the degree of saturation.

FIGURE 7-1 *The effective use of* color *in displays is a strong and helpful partner to increased sales.*
Courtesy of Gimbels Midwest, Inc., Milwaukee, Wis.

Value refers to the range of grays from white through black. (*Tints* are those hues closest to white, and *shades* those hues closest to black.)

Color systems, when not applied, provide little practical knowledge or value. Display people should familiarize themselves with their essentials, but real knowledge comes from actually working with color. We soon learn that each color system is based on a limited conception. For example, the *color wheel* will indicate the approximate color that will result from mixing adjacent hues, but it bears little relationship to prismatic color or that which results from the mixture of colored light.

Many theories have been developed on color. One of the best known is the

Munsell Color Designation System. Munsell recognized a total of 100 different hues around a wheel, starting with a basic five: yellow, red, purple, blue, and green. The mixture of two adjacent hues results in an *intermediate* hue.

The Ostwald System recognizes 24 colors around a wheel. Supporters of this system argue that its four basic colors—yellow, red, blue, and sea-green—are arranged more exactly opposite their true complements than in other systems.[1]

The Munsell and Ostwald systems differ from the well-known color wheel for color mixing that we may recall from our earliest school years. This wheel has three *primary* colors—red, yellow, and blue—and three *secondary* colors—orange, violet, and green—that result from mixing two primaries. Orange results from red and yellow, violet results from red and blue, and green results from blue and yellow. (See insert.)

Chromatic colors are colors such as red, yellow, and blue. They are considered as having color, or hue, because of reflective properties. *Achromatic hues* are in essence neutrals, such as black, white, or grays. They are either totally reflective (unsaturated) or totally absorbent (saturated) in regard to their light properties. In a sense, they have no visual color.

All hues are created by the three (primary) original colors: red, blue, and yellow. These three colors, combined with one another in various proportions, complete the entire spectrum and produce all chromatic colors. Illustrations of their placement on the color wheel, and the other hues that their combination produces, follow.

COLOR SCHEMES

Through the use of a color wheel, such as those appearing in this section, colors may be combined according to their position on the wheel and may then evolve as *color schemes*. These schemes are simply calculated ways that colors may be combined successfully through the use of a formula.

As each color scheme is discussed, it will be considered in terms of how many colors are involved in the scheme, where these colors are positioned on the color wheel, and what changes in value and intensity might be expected in any one color scheme.

MONOCHROMATIC

This color scheme consists of one basic hue. This hue may appear at any point on the color wheel. It appears in from three to five different values and therefore runs the gamut from the full hue to varying tints (pastels) of this hue. Five colors ranging from red to pale pink would constitute a monochromatic color scheme.

[1]Emily Mauger, *Modern Display Techniques* (New York: Fairchild Publication, 1964), p. 51.

ANALOGOUS

An analogous color scheme consists of from three to five or more different hues that are placed consecutively on the color wheel and must include no more than one-third of the wheel. There are few noticeable gaps in the colors represented. Therefore, if an analogous color scheme uses the colors from blue to green, varying values and intensities of all of the hues between blue and green are represented. The changes in these hues in regard to value and intensity may be many and varied and give this color scheme great versatility, yet continuity. Five colors ranging from blue to blue green to pale green and perhaps a yellow green or yellow would constitute an analogous color scheme.

TRIADIC

A triadic color scheme involves three colors. These colors may be any three that are equidistant from one another on the color wheel. Thus, red, blue, and yellow constitute a triadic color scheme. Owing to the wide separation of these colors on the wheel and the fact that they essentially cover the entire range of the wheel, one or more of the colors may undergo changes in value or in intensity to decrease the contrast represented. These changes, however, are not essential.

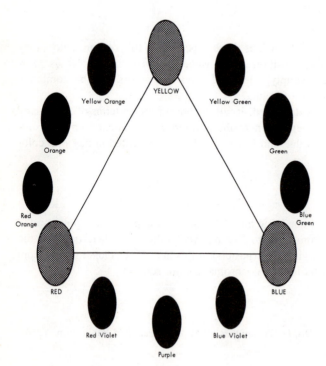

FIGURE 7-2 *Triadic*

COMPLEMENTARY

A complementary color scheme consists of two colors or hues that are exactly opposite one another on the color wheel. Because of their wide contrast, when used together they tend to intensify one another. Thus, when red is used with green, the green appears greener than when it is combined with blue. One or both of the colors may be changed in either value or intensity to avoid too much contrast and color intensification. Green and red could thus be changed in value and intensity respectively and appear pale green and dark red.

SPLIT COMPLEMENTARY

This scheme consists of three hues. One is determined as being the basic hue in the scheme, and the other two are those that appear on either side of the basic hue's complement. The distances between the basic hue's complement and the split complement on either side must be exactly equal. Again, value and intensity changes of any or all of these three colors may be used. Yellow, red violet, and blue violet would constitute a split-complementary color scheme. The split-complementary scheme offers a bit more variety than the complementary scheme.

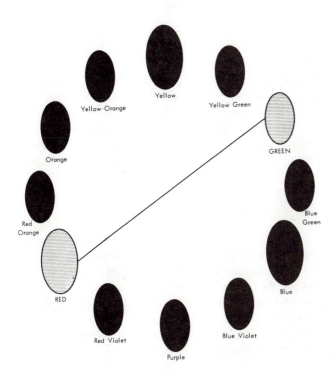

FIGURE 7–3 *Complementary*

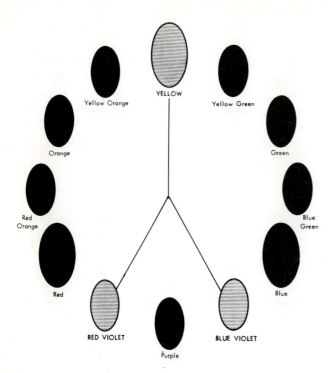

YELLOW

Yellow Orange

Yellow Green

Orange

Green

Red
Orange

Blue
Green

Red

Blue

RED VIOLET

BLUE VIOLET

Purple

FIGURE 7–4 *Split complementary*

DOUBLE COMPLEMENTARY

A double-complementary color scheme consists of four hues, which are any two sets of complementary colors. They may be four colors that are widely separated and appear on each of the four sides of the color wheel, or they may be four colors of which two oppose two others, as in the case of red and orange—red being used as the complement of green and orange as the complement of blue. Because of the wide variety of colors that may be used, changes in both value and intensity often occur to give the scheme more continuity and viewing ease.

TONE ON TONE

A tone-on-tone color scheme consists of two hues that are next to one another on the color wheel with very little space between them, such as green and blue green. The blue green is so close to the green on the blue side of the wheel that almost no hue difference is readily apparent when the viewer glances at the two colors. There is usually no change in either intensity or in value in the use of this scheme. It is used as a subtle device in fashion merchandising with great care and skill.

These schemes may be varied and innovations in them made as you become more skilled in the use of color-combination techniques.

COLOR WHEEL

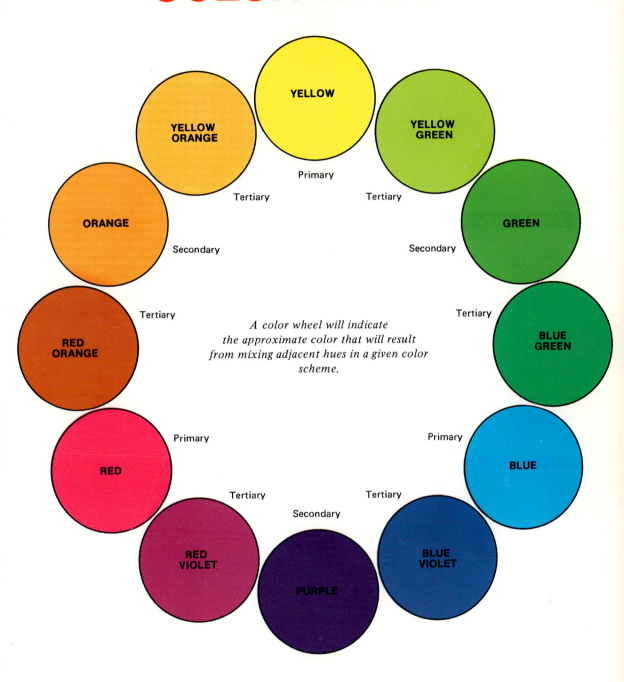

YELLOW

YELLOW ORANGE

YELLOW GREEN

Primary

Tertiary

Tertiary

ORANGE

GREEN

Secondary

Secondary

Tertiary

Tertiary

RED ORANGE

BLUE GREEN

*A color wheel will indicate
the approximate color that will result
from mixing adjacent hues in a given color
scheme.*

Primary

Primary

RED

BLUE

Tertiary

Tertiary

RED VIOLET

Secondary

BLUE VIOLET

PURPLE

A mannequin can set the attitude or atmosphere of a display, such as elegance or quality.

Courtesy of Gimbels Midwest, Inc., Milwaukee, Wis.

An example of an informally balanced display.

Courtesy of Gimbels Midwest, Inc., Milwaukee, Wis.

AMOUNT AND USE OF COLOR

The display person cannot satisfy the color tastes of everyone all the time, but can cultivate the taste of customers gradually and purposefully. Keep in mind that the colors people say they prefer and the ones they actually buy are often entirely different. Tests conducted by a color research institute revealed the following: (1) Of those asked to choose a favorite coffee offered them because of taste, over two-thirds made their differentiation on the basis of color of container. The contents of all three cups were the same, yet the green cup won most acclaim. (2) Over 90 percent of women tasting in a margarine — butter study chose the yellow pat as butter by taste when actually the white pat was butter.

Display workers should learn a few simple rules and study numerous practical examples, keeping records as they go along. The more scientific *facts* you know about color, the better—but do not expect them to teach you taste. Observations of nature and fashion are the most important sources of inspiration in teaching color know-how.

Now that information on color terminology and color schemes has been presented, here is an outline of rules that the display person may use in combining colors in their respective values and intensities within a display. Also presented in Table 7−1 is a chart of suggested background colors that might be employed in a display and the subsequent effects that these backgrounds might have.

RULES REGARDING COLOR IN DISPLAY

1. Use strong contrasts and loud color with care
   a. Although very bright hues command attention at first, they disturb immediately afterwards and distract attention from the merchandise.

TABLE 7-1 Color of Backgrounds

Color of Merchandise	Black Background	White Background	Beige Background	Dark Gray Background
YELLOW	Enhanced in richness	Lightly duller	Warmer	Brighter
RED	Far more brilliant	Darker, purer	Bright, but less intense	Brighter, but loses saturation
BLUE	More luminous	Richer and darker	Little more luminous	Brighter
GREEN	Paler, sharpened	Deepens in value	Takes on yellowish cast	Brightens, gray becomes reddish
ORANGE	More luminous	Darker and redder	Lighter and yellowish	Increases brilliancy
PURPLE	Loses strength and brilliancy	Darker	Brighter, gray becomes greenish	Gray becomes green

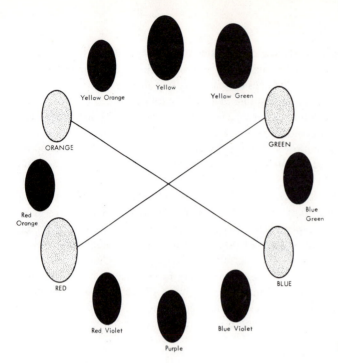

FIGURE 7–5 *Double complementary*

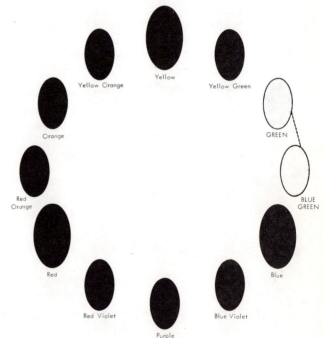

FIGURE 7–6 *Tone on tone*

This display gives the viewer a look of quality, uniqueness, and expense through the use of color, props, and self-selection of merchandise.

Courtesy of Gimbels Midwest, Inc., Milwaukee, Wis.

The effective use of color in displays is a strong and helpful partner to increased sales.

Courtesy of Gimbels Midwest, Inc., Milwaukee, Wis.

Soft goods may be displayed in several different ways, using various props.

Courtesy of Gimbels Midwest, Inc., Milwaukee, Wis.

The pillow week theme gives the feeling that there is a "special" on pillows.
Courtesy of Gimbels Midwest, Inc., Milwaukee, Wis.

The visual merchandising team must work together to produce effective displays.
Courtesy of Gimbels Midwest, Inc., Milwaukee, Wis.

     b. The more intense a hue, the smaller the area it should cover.

     c. The more intense a hue, the softer should be the second hue used in combination with it. Do not combine two or more strong colors that have not been changed in value or intensity.

     d. Do not paint large surfaces in strong colors.

2. Make your color scheme suit the merchandise on display
   a. The color of floors, walls, and background should be either one of the main colors in the merchandise or a neutral shade.
   b. Generally speaking, soft tints should be given preference over saturated hues.

3. The type of merchandise displayed has a bearing on the selection of colors
   a. Low-priced goods are displayed in a color scheme of vivid hue.
   b. The more exclusive types of merchandise, on the other hand, are displayed in a refined color scheme and in color combinations used in the current fashion.

4. Light tints are always a treat for the eye
   a. They appear to deepen the window space.
   b. Therefore, they seemingly increase the size of the window.

5. The opposite is true of dark shades
   a. They seem to bring the background closer.
   b. Therefore, they shorten the window space in the eyes of the spectator.

6. Most colors can be classified as warm or cool
   a. Warm colors include yellow, orange, red, and their combinations with white or black. All these hues impress the eye, enhance the appearance of the merchandise, and optically push it to the front of the display.
   b. Cool colors include blue and green. They appear calm, soothing, and balanced, and they create the illusion of enlarging the window.

7. Contrasts are welcome but dangerous
   a. Beware of clashes.
   b. Confine strong contrasts to small accessories.
   c. Audacious combinations are permissible if taste is preserved.

8. More than two principal colors can be grouped in one display, but proportionately; more care must be taken to achieve harmony.
   a. Most pastels go well together.

In summary, realizing the importance of color in display, the beginning display person should study color schemes created by leading display artists and by fashion designers. Remember that when implementing the effective use of color, it is better to create a simple display in a becoming color scheme than a sophisticated display in a poor color scheme.

Practice in creating displays is the only way to become an effective display person.

SUGGESTED ACTIVITIES

1. Visit your local paint stores or departments and discuss the mixing of paints. This will dramatically emphasize the makeup of colors and should implement the color wheel with practical information—especially if the interviewee will demonstrate the mixing.

2. A review of color use in the local display departments by direct observation will give you some appreciation for and knowledge of color and its application.
3. Using the color-of-backgrounds table as a reference, test the various guidelines listed with various kinds of material. Describe the experiment in writing and be prepared to explain and, if possible, demonstrate it.

EVALUATION

Multiple Choice

1. Which one of the following is a hue?
   a. Pink
   b. Red
   c. Brown
   d. White
2. Which of the following is an element of proportion?
   a. Triadic
   b. Radiation
   c. Pyramid
   d. Texture
3. A tone-on-tone color scheme consists of:
   a. One hue, varying in intensity
   b. One hue, varying in value
   c. Two hues, the same in intensity and value
   d. Three hues next to each other on the wheel
4. The intensity of a hue refers to:
   a. How much white has been added to the hue
   b. How light or dark it is
   c. Where it is on the color wheel
   d. How bright or dull it is
5. The step concept refers to the:
   a. Balance of a display
   b. Proportion of a display
   c. Lighting effect
   d. Setting up of a schedule for a display
6. Continuous line movement refers to:
   a. The rhythm of a display
   b. The point of eye contact
   c. Harmony
   d. Texture
7. Red, yellow, and green are:
   a. The primary colors
   b. The achromatic colors
   c. Chromatic colors
   d. Complementary colors

8. Line, shape, and size refer to:
   a. Shelves and props
   b. Lighting effects
   c. Aspects of harmony
   d. Kinds of balance
9. Perfect symmetry may occur in:
   a. A time-flow chart
   b. Formal balance
   c. The step arrangement
   d. Informal balance
10. Color is involved with:
   a. The presence of light
   b. The absence of light
   c. Both the above
   d. Neither of the above
11. The elements of display include:
   a. Balance
   b. Radiation
   c. Both the above
   d. Neither of the above
12. Display began with:
   a. Surrealism
   b. The fig leaf
   c. The Exposition of Decorative Arts in Paris, 1926
   d. World War I
   e. None of the above
13. Wax dummies were not effective because:
   a. They gave display people hernias
   b. They looked too much like large candles
   c. They lasted forever
   d. All the above
14. Surrealism was triggered by:
   a. Jung
   b. Allport
   c. The Art Expo of 1926
   d. Freud in 1936
   e. None of the above
15. Improvisation in display is:
   a. Always bad
   b. Usually bad
   c. An excuse for no preparation
   d. The core of a display's vitality
   e. None of the above
16. Plagiarism is:
   a. Taboo in display
   b. The core of display philosophy
   c. Permissible, depending on geographic area
   d. Unprofessional

17. Visual merchandising:
    a. Refers to advertising layout
    b. Is a calculated application of esthetics to visual selling
    c. Is essentially different from merchandise display in one or more aspects
    d. All the above
18. Emphasis refers to:
    a. Bright colors only
    b. Initial eye contact
    c. Vitality
    d. An aspect of harmony
    e. An aspect of proportion
19. Harmony deals with:
    a. Space relations
    b. Agreement of parts
    c. Weights
    d. Boundaries
20. Hems are a part of:
    a. Emphasis
    b. Repetition
    c. Lighting
    d. Merchandise
21. Right-to-left diagonal lines are:
    a. Pleasant
    b. Unstable
    c. Rigid
    d. Restful
22. Vertical lines are:
    a. Strong
    b. Feminine
    c. Unstable
    d. Irritating
23. The double reverse curve is sometimes called:
    a. Zigzag
    b. A circle
    c. Double emphasis
    d. A pyramid
24. Radiation:
    a. Has strong vertical features
    b. Is very unbalanced
    c. Is active and dynamic
    d. Is usually formal

Matching

———— PROPORTION

———— RADIATION

———— BLACK

———— EMPHASIS

1. A primary color scheme

2. The state of equipoise between the totals of two sides of an entity

———— SHOWCARD

———— BALANCE

———— ANALOGOUS

———— HARMONY

———— VALUE

———— INTENSITY

———— RHYTHM

———— INFORMAL

———— FORMAL

———— SHADES

———— TRIADIC

3. Achromatic color

4. The agreement between the many parts and aspects of an entity

5. The sunburst effect

6. The equality of ratios, or a relation among quantities

7. Point of eye contact

8. Hues immediately next to one another on the color wheel

9. An element of display

10. Involving the measurement of motion

11. Name given hues when light rays have been blocked out

12. Lightness or darkness of a hue

13. Referring to how much of a hue is still visible to the eye

14. Consisting of a dominant center piece

15. Making use of a strong left-to-right diagonal line with hems

Project Seven: COLOR-WHEEL AND COLOR-SCHEME ANALYSIS

The purpose of this project is to give the student a practical understanding of how the various hues, tints, and shades of the color wheel emerge from the chromatics of red, blue, and yellow (the primary colors) and the achromatics of black and white. In addition, it is intended to give the student experience in combining colors in such a way as to illustrate how each of the seven color schemes mentioned in the text can evolve.

Materials needed:

Eight 12" by 12" showcards

Red, blue, yellow, black, and white tempera paint

Mixing pans

The completed project will include:

A color wheel containing the primary colors, the secondary colors, and the tertiary colors

One showcard illustrating each of the seven color schemes (including various shades and tints of the hues used)

The showcards are to include the following information:

Name of the color scheme

Hues present

An illustration of where they are placed on the color wheel

A chart indicating whether or not each hue used has been changed in value or intensity

Whether the total effect of the scheme is warm or cool

Guidelines
to Lighting

Proper display lighting is vital to selling. It pulls customers' eyes to the merchandise and encourages them to buy. Moreover, it can be used to direct shoppers through the store, urging them to pause and examine displays of featured goods. People buy because they see.

There is no magic about the attraction of proper display lighting. To a great extent, buying decisions are the result of seeing. The shopper's eye is drawn automatically to the brightest thing in its field. Therefore, the lighting on a display should be two to five times stronger than the room lighting.

Consider brightness of detail. Bold checks on white cloth, for example, stand out even in semidarkness. But put the same checks on a piece of black cloth, and what happens? You may have trouble seeing them in the sunlight.

A good rule of thumb is: *The more difficult it is to see detail, the more display light needed.* Yet strong lighting alone will not necessarily tempt customers to buy. Lighting should also have the quality and color that bring our the best features of the merchandise.

The important thing for the manager and merchandiser to keep in mind is that the purpose of display lighting is to call attention to merchandise. Expert display people use light in the same way a musician uses sound. A musician varies the volume to attract attention and manipulates tones to create a mood. Similarly, a display expert varies the amount of light to pull shoppers over to a display, using colored lamps, soft light, and so on, to create a buying mood.

The principles behind the art of light in the home, the store, or the theater are highly technical. However, for display purposes, the analysis of lighting patterns in their simplest form will suffice. The reader should understand that *light is radiant energy reflecting from an object and acting on the retina of the eye to make that object visible. Intensity,* in lighting, *is the degree or amount of that reflection.*

The lighting must be considered in planning a store—beginning with the neon sign out front that identifies the store and going right up the stairways, down the aisles, to the elevators, and back to the front door.

There are three distinct phases of lighting to consider in a discussion of store illumination: *primary, secondary,* and *atmosphere* lighting. (See Figure 8–1.)

1. *Primary Lighting*—Primary lighting supplies the bare essentials of store illumination. Outside, it includes the 150-watt bulbs used as basic window lighting, the marquee lights illuminating the sidewalk for the window shopper, and the lobby ceiling lights. Inside, primary lighting provides general illumination for the store, including lights along the aisles, an

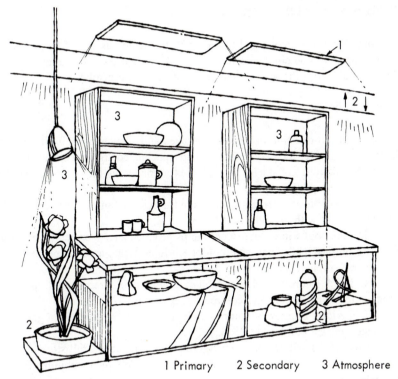

1 Primary   2 Secondary   3 Atmosphere

FIGURE 8–1 *Store lighting*

indicator of an elevator, the light in a stairway, and a directional sign at the fire exit, the office, or the down escalator. This general illumination is the minimum adequate store illumination.

2. *Secondary Lighting*—In itself, primary lighting is inadequate for the specialized showing of merchandise. For this purpose, secondary lighting should be added: Spot- and floodlights augment basic window lighting, brightening the shelves, the cases, the counters, and the merchandise so the customer's eye is attracted. In this second phase of store illumination, lighting begins to function as a definite sales force. Even dresses hanging in stock areas, or aprons on a counter, become more appealing to the customer when illuminated. Besides selling the store, lighting is now selling the contents of the store. Secondary store illumination includes *downlighting* from the ceiling, *showcase lighting,* and *valance lighting.*

3. *Atmosphere Lighting*—The final element in the store lighting pattern is atmosphere lighting. This is the phase that plays light against shadow to create the distinctive effect in specific displays. It is atmosphere lighting that concerns the display person most directly. In the windows, color filters, pinpoint spotlights, and black lighting may be used to create dramatic effects. Inside the store, atmosphere lighting is used in featured displays.[1]

[1]Emily Mauger, *Modern Display Techniques* (New York: Fairchild Publications, 1964), p. 53.

LIGHT SOURCES AS SELLING TOOLS

Customers can be encouraged to buy with the judicious use of lamps. It is up to the display person to obtain the desired effect. Because present-day lamps are economical, anyone can afford the variety necessary for effective display.

FLUORESCENT LAMPS

Fluorescent lamps come in various wattages and sizes and are used for general room lighting, large-area display lighting, and specialized lighting on shelves and showcases. A wide range of shades is available for enhancing the colors of merchandise and the atmosphere of the store.

Warm white and deluxe warm white fluorescent lamps create a *warm* atmosphere and blend well with incandescent lamps.

Deluxe cool white fluorescent lamps produce a *cool* or neutral environment that blends with daylight. They give colors a bright, clear, natural appearance and flatter customers, employees, and store decor.

Colored fluorescent lamps—blue, green, cool green, gold, pink, and red—produce dramatic effects and colored backgrounds.

Ultraviolet fluorescent lamps can be used in areas of reduced general light level to create unusual *black-light* displays.

Caution: If only fluorescent lighting is used, the overall store atmosphere may appear dull and uninteresting. This can be avoided by combining flourescent and incandescent light.

INCANDESCENT LAMPS

Incandescent lamps have sharply defined beams that are easily directed to emphasize merchandise. They come in a great variety of types, shapes, beams, wattages, and colors.

Reflector lamps are most widely used for spotlighting interior displays. The reflectors are sealed in and never need cleaning. They are available in 75, 100, 150, and 200 watts and in spot and flood beams. For higher intensities, 300-watt lamps are available to produce spot, medium flood, and wide flood patterns.

Color spot lamps of 150 watts produce concentrated beams of amber, green, blue, yellow, and red light. They can be used at increased distances from the merchandise.

Cool reflector lamps are good to reduce deterioration of perishable displays and fading or discoloration of merchandise, as well as to boost customer and clerk comfort. A dichroic coating on the built-in reflector removes most of the heat from the light beam yet retains high light output and good beam control. Smart, decorative lamps—in 10- to 100-watt sizes and in a variety of finishes, shapes, and colors—can add sparkle to your displays. For example, Early American chimney lamps lend colonial charm to a display of wigs.

The tungsten-halogen lamp is ideal for lighting many window and wall displays because it is small yet powerful. A 250-watt lamp is not much bigger than a cigarette and delivers a beam of intense light. It can be used in compact, inexpensive fixtures. This type of lamp resists moisture and has a self-cleaning action.

The white metal halide lamp features beam control, long life, and excellent color rendition. It gives a natural daylight beam that can be used for general lighting as well as display. Certain phosphor-coated mercury lamps that flatter red colors may also be used.

Because of their lower lamp efficiency, shorter life, and high heat load, incandescent lamps are not recommended for general lighting where cost is an important factor.

LIGHTING TIPS FOR SPECIFIC MERCHANDISE

1. Use large-area lighting fixtures plus incandescent downlighting to avoid heavy shadows when displaying major appliances and furniture.
2. Use general diffuse or overall lighting, accented with point-type spotlights to emphasize the beauty of china, glass, home accessories, and giftware.
3. Bring out the sparkle and luster of hardware, toys, auto accessories, highly polished silver, and other metalware by using a blend of general light and concentrated light sources—spotlights.
4. Use concentrated beams of high-brightness incandescent sources to add brilliant highlights to jewelry, gold and silver, or cut glass.
5. Highlight the colors, patterns, and textures of rugs, carpets, upholstery, heavy drapes, and bedspreads by using oblique directional lighting plus general low-intensity overhead lighting.
6. Heighten the appeal of menswear by using a cool blend of flourescent and incandescent—with fluorescent predominating.
7. Highlight womenswear—especially the bright, cheerful colors and patterns—by using natural white fluorescents blended with tungsten-halogen.
8. Bring out the tempting colors of meats, fruits, and vegetables by using fluorescent lamps rich in red energy, including the deluxe cool white type. Cool reflector incandescent lamps may also be used for direct-type lighting.

COMMON LIGHTING DEFINITIONS

Ballast: The electrical device that supplies the proper voltage and currency necessary to start and operate a discharge lamp. The most common is the electromagnetic type, which is typically the "little black box" mounted inside the luminaire. Certain lamps are equipped with "solid-state" ballasts. See *Luminaire.*

Barn Door: An accessory used with spotlights to control the spread of a beam of light. It usually attaches in front of the spotlight in the color frame guide and has four adjustable flaps or "doors" (one to either side, one on top, and one on the bottom) that can be maneuvered to control the direction of the light or completely block off the light in any direction. Sheets of colored frosted gelatin or plastic and spun-glass diffusers can be used with this device.

Bee Lights: Miniature screw-base-type electric bulbs of very low wattage, such as are used in strings of 20 or 36 for Christmas decorating; tiny tubular or globe-shaped replaceable bulbs.

Black Light: A special ultraviolet light bulb, incandescent or flourescent, that will cause surfaces treated with ultraviolet paint or the like to glow in the dark. The black light is directed onto the treated surfaces, and the darker the area, the more intense and more brilliant the treated objects or surfaces appear. A theatrical device.

Border Light: A striplight hanging from an overhead batten, pipe, or ceiling grid and used to produce general overall lighting in a window or on a stage. See *Striplights*.

Canopy: An enclosure or cap, placed between the stem of the fixture and the outlet box in the ceiling, that conceals the wire connections in this gap.

Chase Lights: A series of lamps that flash on and off in a set pattern, reminiscent of the lights that seem to "run" around theater marquees. It usually comes with its own timing device that sets and controls the flashing or "chase" pattern.

Cove Lighting: A form of indirect lighting. The lighting source in the area is concealed from below by a recess, cove, cornice, or baffle, and sometimes by a partially dropped ceiling. The light is reflected by the ceiling or wall. A soft, subtle way of lighting an area or a wall.

Dimmer: A mechanism for changing the intensity of light in a given area by means of cutting down on the amount of electric current passing through the electrical wires to the lamps. The resistance dimmer is the only one that will work on direct current (D.C.) whereas autotransformer, electronic resistance, electronic, and magnetic amplifier dimmers will work on alternating currents (A.C.).

Downlight: A light fixture with a reflecting surface, shade, or shield that directs the beam or spread of light downward toward the floor area rather than toward the ceiling.

Flasher: A device that screws into a light-bulb socket before the lamp is inserted and causes the light bulb to flash on and off by interfering with the flow of electric current. Sometimes a set of miniature light bulbs will come with a flasher bulb that causes the current breaks.

Flicker Bulb: A candle-shaped bulb with a fiilment that flickers and spurts, mechanically simulating a candle flame.

Floodlight: An electric lamp or bulb that throws a broad spread or wash of light over a wide area. Floodlights are available in varying wattages, from 75 watts on up.

Indirect Lighting: A lighting arrangement in which the light is directed to the ceiling or any other reflective surface, from which it is bounced back to illuminate the general area, rather than being directed straight down to the area below. See *Cove Lighting*.

Insulator: A nonconductor of electricity, like rubber, porcelain, asbestos, and some plastics. The insulator is used around electrical conductors (copper wire) as a protective coating.

Lamp: The complete light-source unit, which usually consists of a light-generating element (a filament or arc tube), the accessory hardware, the enclosure or envelope (usually glass) for the assorted parts, and the base that fits into the socket; an electric light bulb.

Luminaire: The complete lighting unit (from the French word for "light" or "lamp"). It includes the lamp socket, housing, frame, holder, reflector, shield, and so on.

Primary Lighting: The basic, most elementary and elemental lighting of a store or selling area. Usually it does not include special lighting effects—spots, floods, filters, washes, and so on—and is almost devoid of any sort of atmosphere or mood.

Projectors: The projection process consists of a light source, objects or slides to be projected, and the surface or screen upon which the image is projected. The projector is the light source, and the image may be projected by lens, for a sharper effect, or by shadow, which is less complicated. Front projection places the projector in front of an opaque screen (downstage); rear projection places the projector behind a transluscent screen (backstage). In either case, a certain amount of space is required between the projector and the screen.

Reflector: Polished or mirrored surface that is used to redirect light in a desired direction, or onto a specific area; a baffle or screen used to reflect heated air.

Secondary Lighting: The spots, floods, filters, washes, and so on, that add depth, dimension, and atmosphere to a lighting plan; the lighting beyond the basic or primary lighting plan. See *Primary Lighting*.

Showcase Lamps: Long, thin, sausage-shaped incandescent lamps that are available in 25-, 40-, and 60-watt strengths.

Specific Illumination: Form-revealing, highlighting, and attention-getting lighting that focuses the viewer's attention on a specific object or area. This form of lighting is usually accomplished with spotlights and/or concentrated beams of light, sometimes through a color filter.

Strip Lighting: Long lines of exposed fluorescent fixtures on a ceiling.

Striplights: A general term that includes border lights, footlights, cyclorama, border, and backing striplights. Striplights usually consist of rows of individual reflectors, each containing one lamp and a round glass color medium that covers the entire mouth of the reflector. They are often wired in three or four circuits, for the primary colors (red, blue, green), and possibly one for white.

Switchboard: A portable or fixed panel with switches, dimmers, and so on, that controls all the lamps and outlets in a window or group of windows, or for a stage. By means of the switchboard, it is possible to turn specific lights on or off without having to climb or reach for them.

Swivel Socket: A socket with a 360-degree swivel joint between the screw-in socket end and the receptacle that receives the lamp or bulb. It is possible, when the lamp is screwed into the socket, to rotate and direct that lamp or bulb to any direction—up or down, and to all sides. The swivel socket sometimes comes with an extension pipe before the swivel device.

Track Lighting: A channel or track, usually attached to a ceiling or ledge, that is electrically wired and plugged into a source of electric current, The 4-, 6-, or 8-foot lengths of channel will receive assorted spotlights and floodlights, in decorative holders or housings. This is selective lighting, since it is possible to move these lamps about on the length of channel, turn the individual lamps on and off as needed, and direct the light where one wants it, thus making changes in light emphasis.

INTERIOR FEATURE DISPLAYS

Extra lighting is the key in building feature displays—ones that sell new items, remind customers of products that carry a high markup, or help to move closeouts quickly. Feature displays can be made with regular merchandising fixtures, such as wall cases, or with movable merchandising fixtures, such as tables. The secret is using light that is from two to two and a half times stronger than the light you use on your regular displays.

In using such spots of brightness, it is important to vary their location from time to time to give customers something new to look at.

Thought should be given to using your wall fixtures for promotional displays. Shelves, niches, and wall showcases can be made to do an extra selling job by the judicious use of extra lighting.

Start by locating lighting fixtures far enough in front of the merchandise to provide effective brightness on all vertical surfaces. Vary the lamp wattage or the quantity of lighting fixtures to project two to two and a half times the light used for a regular wall display.

An example would be a display of summer dresses in a wall case. One store uses deluxe natural white reflector-type fluorescent lamps for regular display in the wall case. By the addition of 250-watt tungsten-halogen lamps, the case becomes a promotional display, producing a sunshine effect that reminds customers of the season. In addition, these lamps bring out color in a way that appeals to shoppers.

In another store, the owner-manager makes sure that the bottom row of suits in a double-tiered rack is not neglected. He uses aperture-type fluorescent lamps to throw a beam of light on the coat sleeves on the lower tier.

If you want customers to look into showcases, light them internally. Small-diameter fluorescent lamps are used because they bring out merchandise quality and produce a minimum of heat. However, reflectorized tubular incandescent lamps may be used in smaller showcases. There are two types of artificial light sources, incandescent and fluorescent. In the incandescent, electric energy flows through a very thin wire (filament) that resists the flow of energy. This causes the filament to heat up and, consequently, to glow. The heat that is produced can, in confined, unventilated areas, be a definite fire hazard. Incandescent light is flexible in use and therefore very useful in special effects. This type of light is always used with a fitting or reflector, unless it is used in lines or batteries. Incandescent lamps give a warmer effect but are less diffused and much less economical than fluorescent.

Fluorescent lighting is actually electrical energy causing phosphors to glow in a tube. It is very economical and provides shadowless light that is valuable for general background or ceiling illumination. It is cool and produces little heat, making it good for small, enclosed areas. However, it does tend to make some objects look unpleasant and cannot be focused or projected. Maximum efficiency is obtained when the tube is placed next to a flat white surface that reflects the light beams.

SHOW-WINDOW LIGHTING

The old saying, that a show window mirrors what is inside the store, is still true. Properly lighted, window displays can help sell specific products or ideas that promote the store's image.

Display lighting in show windows of open-front stores is fairly simple. The lights in such windows—and store interiors—should be strong enough to overcome the reflections from outside objects such as parked cars and buildings. At night, additional light on overhead marquees and projecting cornices can make the window area look larger.

A high-level general illumination is the first requirement for a closed-back window. An exception would be the attempt to achieve dramatic effects, perhaps by using some spotlights in a darkened window.

Massed window displays are often lighted with overhead fluorescents that are supplemented by closely spaced clear incandescent lamps. Metal halide lamps can also be used. They give a highly contrasting light with many of the best display features of combination fluorescent-incandescent systems. Certain phosphor-coated mercury lamps that flatter red colors may also be used.

The more direct lighting of tungsten-halogen lamps is especially effective on high-style displays. Dichroic and other color filters may be used to produce colored light from lamps with white beams. Eye-catching mobile color effects can be provided by automatic dimming of switching cycles. Center each principal display between two or more adjustable lights and have extra illumination for emphasizing the display and for overcoming reflections on the glass.

Use miniature portable spotlights to accent small display areas, price cards, and specific items in a massed display. Compact footlights help relieve shadows near the bottom of vertical displays.

Fixtures for special display lighting can take many forms. Some downlights can be almost completely hidden in the ceiling. Other exposed, bullet-type units are available in attractive geometric shapes that flatter a store's architectural decor. Flexibility is the feature of many fixtures. They will accept a wide variety of lamp wattages and beam patterns. For rapid rearrangement, some fixtures can be plugged

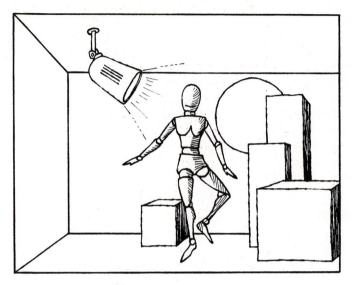

VERTICAL DISPLAY   All items are
covered with lighting from one side
or the other.

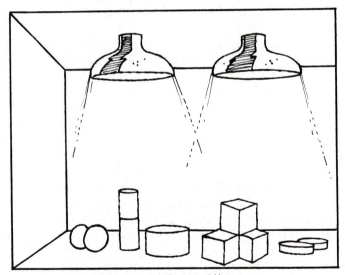

HORIZONTAL DISPLAY   All items are
covered with lighting from the top view.

FIGURE 8–2 *"Wash"*

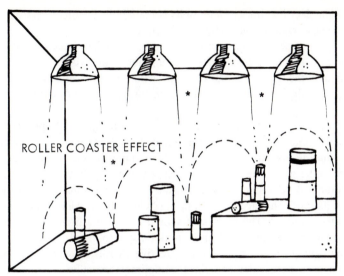

ROLLER COASTER EFFECT

*Incorrect: Shadow gaps not covered
by lighting beams.

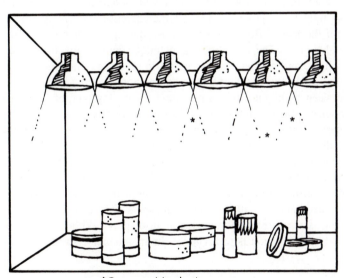

*Correct: No shadow gaps.

FIGURE 8–3 *Correct and incorrect "wash" technique*

directly into an electrical track. Other units contain built-in silicon rectifiers or special ballasts that allow wide-range dimming of light output.

Display windows act like mirrors. A mirror has a dark backing material, a layer of silvering, and a pane of clear glass. The interior of the window area acts as a dark background and the glass as the silvering with the sun reflecting. To overcome reflections, more light must be coming from inside the window than is hitting the outside.

Now let us discuss the lighting of the mannequin. A prime requisite is naturalness. The main spot should come from overhead. (From below, it would give an unreal, unflattering appearance.) It should be as far from the mannequin as possible and as close to the glass line as can be managed. One spotlight is not enough to light one mannequin. (A spotlight concentrates the light. It has more sparkle and punch in the center of its rays. The face of the lamp is of clear glass.) Mannequins are usually at an angle to the window. The main spot should be a white light. Aim it to cover the main part of the mannequin. Next, use a pink pinspot to highlight the face with color. Also, on the ceiling, a side spot is very effective. It fills in deep, dark shadows and often can be used as a color spot in a complimentary color on merchandise. For back-wall color lighting, or to hit accessories or a showcard, or to fill in shadows, a spot on the side wall of the display is very handy.

Many stores have show windows filled with merchandise. In these windows, it is necessary to light these large amounts of merchandise effectively yet interestingly. This calls for the use of floodlights that wash the light over a broad area through a frosted, pebbled glass. The wash lighting technique completely covers every nook and cranny with light, and no merchandise is lost in shadows. The common fault in wash lighting is the roller-coster effect that is due to poor spacing of lamps. This creates shadows between highlights. It is a mountain-and-valley type of light. To overcome this, overlapping reflector lights must be spaced correctly.

In determining the proper placement of lamps, one must consider the merchandise to be displayed. Stores promoting many items in one window, where the merchandise is generally on a flat plane and there is a great deal of it, use floodlights and the wash lighting technique. An occasional spotlight can be used to pick out some special items. Vertical display, using mannequins with both back walls and side walls covered with merchandise, calls for floods and spots from the ceiling at the glass line.

Lighting is the most important factor in display. Without it, the merchandise cannot be seen. Its function is to highlight the merchandise so that it will sell.

SUMMARY

The objective of proper lighting is to make it impossible for a shopper not to see the merchandise.

Colored lights are used to emphasize the color of merchandise, create atmosphere, attract attention, or emphasize desirable undertones. When colored lights are used, they should be more intense, because darker colors tend to "swallow" light. The most versatile colored light fixture is an ordinary lamp with a filter wheel that can be turned to show a desired color.

Lighting methods include pinpointing, spotlighting, floodlighting, diffused lighting, and indirect lighting.

Directional control will improve displays by eliminating glare, bringing out textures and patterns, concentrating light for emphasis, producing effective shadows, and eliminating unwanted shadows.

Project Eight: CONSTRUCTION OF OPEN SHADOW-BOX DISPLAYS
WITH HEIGHT AND SIDES EXTENDED

This project is to give the student experience in constructing a shadow-box display with four or fewer sides.

Each student will be assigned a shadow box and may remove either the top or sides or both if he or she selects to do so. Therefore, the problem will consist of constructing a display in a shadow box with one to four surfaces. Merchandise may now be extended above the height of the sides and may also be allowed to drape below the base of the shelf.

Merchandise and props will be selected for the display as soon as the shelf has been prepared. A method of lighting will be selected and a showcard prepared.

The display is now ready for construction according to the principles of design, upon which it will be evaluated. After the student has completed construction, viewed the display from the front, the right, and the left, and made any revisions felt

DISPLAY CONSTRUCTION CHECK LIST

1. Decide on merchandise to be displayed.   _____
2. Select display area.   _____
3. Fill in display sketch sheet.   _____
4. Lay out the showcard.   _____
5. Produce the showcard.   _____
6. Arrange to obtain merchandise (use Loan
   Sheet if necessary).   _____
7. Clean and prepare display area.   _____
8. Accumulate props.   _____
9. Put the display in the display area.
10. Evaluate the display (use Evaluation Sheet).   _____
11. Return merchandise.   _____
12. Return props.   _____
13. Clean display area.   _____
14. File materials on display in project packet for use
    in final portfolio.   _____

SKETCH SHEET

Name _____

Name _____

Name _____

Sketch # _____

(Display Area #)

S K E T C H

Materials from Lab: _____ (Numbers)

_____ (Numbers)

_____ (Numbers)

Outside of lab materials: _____

Merchandise: _____

Showcard theme: (Actual words to appear on card)

_____

Signature of Instructor:

_____

necessary, it will be ready for student-instructor evaluation. It is important that before evaluation by the instructor, the student evaluate the display and be flexible enough to totally revise it based on that criticism.

Construction time should be limited to one and a half hours, with six to ten minutes for evaluation.

After the display is evaluated, it is disassembled, and the props are returned to the prop room. The merchandise should be carefully inspected and returned to its source. The display shelf should be cleaned and prepared for use by another student.

DISPLAY EVALUATION SHEET

Criteria	Possible Points	Points	Comments
Subject—Its appropriateness in the store situation	10		
Neatness and preparation of the display area	5		
Message and total effect	5		
Elements: Props Shelf Lighting Showcard Merchandise	10		
Organization and planning: Promptness Sketch	5		
Principles: Emphasis Harmony Balance Rhythm Proportion	10		
Color—Theme and execution	5		

9

Promotional and Institutional Displays

theory and application

A store may follow any of three basic promotional policies, and there are three display styles that go along with these policies.

THE PROMOTIONAL STORE

The first type of store is *promotional*—committed to a policy of aggressive promotion. This store needs a large sales volume to exist. It generally features its prices and makes very little profit per unit of merchandise sold.

The most common type of display is that of the promotional store. It usually features several items of merchandise at once, backed up by lighting, signs, props, and traditional display techniques, because many items must be sold if a reasonable profit is to be made. This store's advertising and displays customarily deal with only *physical merchandise*.

THE NONPROMOTIONAL STORE

The nonpromotional store employs only very selective advertising, and its sales promotion techniques are subtle. It displays far less merchandise than the promotional store but uses a great deal of *institutional display*.[1]

There are two categories of institutional displays: One is the *service display*, in which only incidental mention is made of merchandise; service, special features, or facilities of the store are featured. The other type is the *prestige display*, which contains merchandise but has great fashion significance.[2]

Institutional displays create customer loyalty and goodwill, building a reputation for the store. It is difficult to measure their effectiveness, however, because they do not produce direct sales of merchandise, as does a window featuring, say, a specific dress.

Most industrial concerns use institutional displays to get the name of the company to the public. They set up promotional or merchandise displays mainly when working with distributors or entering trade shows.

Institutional displays present a special challenge, because the theme becomes all-important, as do appropriate props and signs. (See Figures 9–1, 9–2, and 9–3.)

[1]Charles M. Edwards, Jr., and Russell A. Brown, *Retail Advertising and Sales Promotion* (Englewood Cliffs, N.J.: Prentice-Hall, 1959), pp. 156–57.
[2]*Ibid.*, p. 161.

FIGURE 9–1 *A service institutional display—windows using antique clothes from a Museum of Science and Industry (for a silk promotion).*
Compliments of Chas. A. Stevens & Co.

FIGURE 9–2 *It is institutional in nature and has both service and prestige overtones. A window to promote a designer and her appearance.*
Compliments of Chas. A. Sstevens & Co.

FIGURE 9–3 *Example of institutional advertising with prestige intent.*
Compliments of Carson, Pirie, Scott & Company.

These displays must be handled carefully, so that they are not submerged in signs and meaningless props.

THE SEMIPROMOTIONAL STORE

The policies of many business establishments fall between the promotional and the nonpromotional. They use prestige and service institutional displays, but also merchandise displays featuring regular-price-line items, special-purchase items, and sales merchandise. These stores are said to have a *semipromotional* policy.

The semipromotional display follows a middle course between those of promotional and nonpromotional stores. It must appeal to both bargain hunters and regular customers who look for some service and prestige promotion.[3]

DISPLAY THEMES

Almost any establishment can take advantage of themes for displays of an institutional, promotional, or semipromotional nature. The list of themes is endless, but here are a few suggestions:

January White Sale	Academy Awards
Hawaiian Sale	Weddings
Back-to-School	Births

[3]*Ibid.*, p. 157.

Lincoln's Birthday
Forecast: Winter Weather
New Year's Resolutions
Easter
Independence Day
Thanksgiving
Halloween
Chinese New Year
Ground Hog Day
Christmas
Jewish holidays
George Washington's
   Birthday
Valentine Day
Memorial Day
Lenten season
Fall-Summer-Winter-Spring
Mardi Gras
Octoberfest
National Cherry Month
National Egg Month
Benjamin Franklin's birthday
In Like a Lion—Out Like a Lamb
   (March)
Spring Housecleaning
Ecology
Church holidays
Seasonal foods
Election Year

Senior Citizens' Month
Grand Opening
Inventory Sale
Going-out-of-Business
Gardening Season
Mother's Day
Father's Day
School graduation
Research for disease cure
Special foods
Fishing
Boating
Dairy Month
Sports (baseball, football,
   basketball)
Honor the Veteran
Cooking
Fall Fix-up Time
Auto tune-up
Floral events
Safety Week
Travel
Gifts
Bicycle promotion
Foreign Fair promotion
Musical Fair promotion
Types of clothing (swimwear, skiing,
   and so on)
American Cotton Week

Hundreds of ideas can stem from just one of these themes, and many more could be added to the list. The display person's job is to effectively and creatively combine display principles and procedures with the chosen theme according to the display policy of the store.

SUGGESTED ACTIVITIES

1. Make arrangements with one of the retailers or industrialists in your city or nearby so that you may visit a trade show where many promotional displays will be presented. Evaluate and observe these institutional display techniques and report your observations to the class.

2. Make an appointment with the display director of a large nearby department store, individually or as a group, and obtain information concerning its largest annual, institutional, all-store promotion, in regard to prop sources, prop construction, special animation, lighting effects, and so on.
3. Individually or as a small group, put an institutional window in your downtown area promoting some widely promoted event such as American Education Week or National DECA Week. Several groups may put in several downtown windows with the effect of a total campaign. This project can also be combined with the efforts of an advertising class.
4. Make an institutional window from signs alone. Use what you have learned about design principles, lighting, and placement in completing the display.

Project Nine: CONSTRUCTION OF PINNED, FLAT-SURFACED DISPLAYS

This project is designed to give the student experience in pinning merchandise to a flat surface to create an effective three-dimensional display. The surfaces may be bulletin boards, hanging metal or wooden art forms, metal screening devices, or other common flat surfaces found in a retail store. An entire wall may be considered.

Individual students—or small groups of students, depending on the magnitude of the display—may be assigned to each area. Soft goods are the best subject for pinned displays, because they tend to be light and flexible. However, any merchandise and any theme may be selected by the student. Students will be expected to create an effective display, including all the display elements on the selected flat surface.

As soon as the surface has been selected, suitable merchandise, along with appropriate props, will be assembled. A method of lighting will be decided upon and a showcard prepared.

DISPLAY CONSTRUCTION CHECK LIST

1. Decide on merchandise to be displayed. _____
2. Select display area. _____
3. Fill in display sketch sheet. _____
4. Lay out the showcard. _____
5. Produce the showcard. _____
6. Arrange to obtain merchandise (use Loan Sheet if necessary). _____
7. Clean and prepare display area. _____
8. Accumulate props. _____
9. Put the display in the display area.
10. Evaluate the display (use Evaluation Sheet). _____
11. Return merchandise. _____
12. Return props. _____
13. Clean display area. _____
14. File materials on display in project packet for use in final portfolio. _____

SKETCH SHEET

Name _____

Name _____

Name _____

Sketch # _____

(Display Area #)

S K E T C H

Materials from Lab: _____ (Numbers)

_____ (Numbers)

_____ (Numbers)

Outside of lab materials: _____

Merchandise: _____

Showcard theme: (Actual words to appear on card)

_____

Signature of Instructor:

_____

     The display is now ready for construction according to design principles. A pinned display must be evaluated from the front, the right, and the left, and from behind if it is on a transparent or perforated surface such as a screen. If the screen is used, the student may wish to do back-to-back displays using both sides of it. When the display has been prepared and viewed from all angles, it is ready for student-instructor evaluation.

     Generally, construction time of pinned displays is individually determined, because areas may range from entire fabric-covered walls to small bulletin-boards. A student who has selected to work individually with a very small surface may be

Group # _____

Area _____

Name _____

Grade _____

DISPLAY EVALUATION SHEET

Criteria	Possible Points	Points	Comments
Subject—Its appropriateness in the store situation	10		
Neatness and preparation of the display area	5		
Message and total effect	5		
Elements: Props Shelf Lighting Showcard Merchandise	10		
Organization and planning: Promptness Sketch	5		
Principles: Emphasis Harmony Balance Rhythm Proportion	10		
Color—Theme and execution	5		

MERCHANDISING/PROP LOAN SHEET

The Visual Merchandising class at _____ School is in the process of constructing displays as part of their class activities. The students will be able to practice the various visual merchandising principles, procedures, and techniques better if they have a variety of display projects. Therefore, please loan them the materials as explained in the attached Project Sheet.

The student has the responsibility of caring for, using, and returning all of the materials. However, please understand that they will be used in actual displays.

Thank you again for assisting the student in receiving a practical learning experience.

Sincerely,

_____

Instructor's Name

assigned more than one pinned display to complete the assignment. Therefore, the total display effort of the student should involve approximately one to one and a half hours, leaving ten to fifteen minutes for student-instructor evaluation.

After the display is prepared and evaluated, it is disassembled and the props are returned to the prop room. The surface may remain as a permanent part of the display or store area. Merchandise should be carefully inspected and returned to its source. The display surface should be checked so that it is ready for the next student.

10

Visual Merchandising Policies and Procedures

people/ processes/ ideas

The field of display is here to stay. That is a well-established fact. It is gaining in size, reputation, and quality as it meets the demands of the more educated consumer.

Because the primary purpose of display is to sell an item, an idea, or a service, the average person can hardly spend a day without coming in contact with display in one form or another. The field is not limited to retail department stores and specialty shops, but has spread to television and motion picture studios, and to industrial and commercial firms.

Because of this growth, the call for skilled display artists is increasing daily. The well-trained display person can even set up shop as a freelance without incurring the high costs usually required to go into business.

The person who wishes to enter this challenging field faces such questions as:

What preparation will I need?

What will I do?

With whom will I work?

Are there opportunities for advancement?

Some of these questions, if not all, can be answered by interviewing display midmanagement personnel, such as display directors, department managers, and management trainees. As an attempt to bring the career world to you, here is a representative example of retail display policy as provided by Charles Stevens & Company of Chicago. (Keep in mind that the policies mentioned may change from store to store and city to city.)

STORE POLICY, DISPLAY

Being a woman's shop located on State Street between Field's and Carson's, we are in one of the busiest retailing districts in the United States. Due to the fact that we rate as a very high specialty shop and compete with the top department and women's stores in the city and throughout the country, we are presented with certain problems.

There are regulations and systems we must abide by to produce the windows we need in order to continue to be a high-rated specialty store. The most important items come from our store creed.

All promotion must stem from merchandise. Merchandise comes first, then promotion. With this in mind, our fashion coordinator travels to New York two or sometimes three times a year. In New York, she is brought up to date on the latest looks and accessories available. She also works with our buyers and has, on her return, a wide scope of what looks and merchandise we will be receiving in our stocks during the coming months.

Working with this knowledge and with the written material received from such sources as *Vogue, Mademoiselle, Tobe,* and our Atkins buying office, she then schedules a meeting with the display director, and together they develop a three- to four-month plan of window themes. This plan is then presented to the promotions committee (which meets monthly) for approval. Changes may be made at this time due to last-minute changes in arrival dates and cancellations of merchandise. On certain occasions, such as Christmas or a "one-color" promotion, buyers will be notified well in advance to buy pieces especially for windows. After the promotions committee has given its approval of the themes, the fashion coordinator and display director call a meeting with the display staff. At this time, they go over each window theme, dates, and a background into the type of merchandise that will be used during that particular two-week promotion. At the conclusion of this meeting, the display department should have a good base to start working on props and backgrounds for windows.

In order to convert the themes into working windows, the display department has to take many things into consideration, such as, will the props and background give adequate coverage without overshadowing or blocking the merchandise? The merchandise is the most important part of the window, props and backgrounds secondary. Will the props work with all types and styles of merchandise being shown? Our windows are set up in such a way that we are showing twelve to thirteen departments in one promotion, with merchandise ranging from the Designer's Shop, Junior Sportswear, Budget Shop, to Half-Sizes. Backgrounds must be general enough to work well with all departments.

With the points above in mind, the display staff, with the guidance of the display director, start to work each theme out. Ideas are presented, some are set up in a mock window in the department, changed, added to, or rejected. The cost factor is also very important. Many good ideas are eliminated because of their cost. The ability of the staff is also important. This is where the guidance of the display director comes into the picture. If he feels he does not have the budget or people capable of carrying out an idea, he recommends that a more suitable idea be selected and developed. In some cases, a good idea may not conform with the look or image we wish to present to the public. Here again, the director is responsible for making sure that the windows reflect the image and personality of the store. To the customer, the windows are the eyes of the store. They are the first thing seen and, therefore, shape one's impression of the store. They reflect the feeling of the store, its tastes and moods. They should be inviting without being misleading.

Our areas (window display and fashion coordination) are always open to change. Although we continually try different ways of merchandising and trimming, at the present we find that the policy above works well for our store and our situation.

DISPLAY PERSONNEL

THE DISPLAY DIRECTOR

The display director is responsible for all windows and display interiors in all stores. He does the buying and distributing of all display props and materials. He interviews and hires his own staff. He plans his budget, a three-month plan, and staff requirements. He works with buyers and branch-store managers on special displays or problems. He also works very closely with Store Planning on new stores and shops, buying mannequins and props to fit with the planned decor. He travels to New York to buy new props and mannequins and collect new ideas that could be adapted to his home stores. He must keep aware of new trends and looks and make his staff aware of them also.

ASSISTANT DISPLAY DIRECTOR

The assistant display director, in the case of our operation, handles the branch-store displays. He works with the display director in selecting props and hiring his help. He runs his end of the display operation from a branch store and has his own crew and workshop. He also handles some of the warehousing of props (cataloguing and storage). He assists the display director in large interior and window trims (main-floor displays and Christmas windows). He is responsible for the trucking of props to the different branches. He works with branch-store managers on problems or special displays.

DISPLAY DESIGNERS (40-HOUR WEEK)

In our operation, this consists at present of a boy and a girl, although it could be two girls or even two boys, depending on the ability of those hired. It is up to the display designers to take the themes and turn them into working windows. Working with the display director, they develop an idea and carry it through to the final stages of the window. They are responsible for putting it in the window and the look of the finished product.

MANNEQUIN DRESSERS (40-HOUR WEEK)

Mannequin dressers work with the assistant fashion coordinator in dressing the interior mannequins as well as the window mannequins. In the area of window mannequins, they pull and put together the mannequins to fit each piece of merchandise. This includes the right leg and arm positions, the right wig and the right facial look to best display the merchandise. The mannequins should always have the right fashion look to convey the message to the customer of how we feel this particular garment should be worn and with what accessories. Mannequin dressers should know about the newest looks, hair styles, etc. They should also be able to pin and fit the clothes to the mannequins to give the right look and proportion. The job of a mannequin dresser in a store such as ours is an extremely important one.

ACCESSORY NICHE TRIMMER (40-HOUR WEEK)

Accessory niches usually tie in with the window backgrounds, and the person who does niches works with the display designers in working out a background that will be suited to displaying small accessory items and still work with the rest of the background. He or she must be able to drape and display small accessory goods to show them at their best. There are many small, time-consuming displays, and the person in this position must be blessed with good patience.

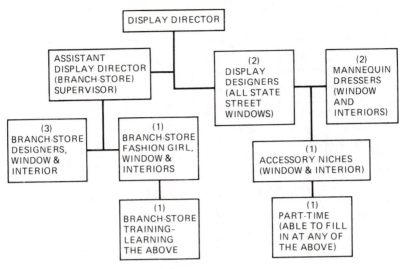

FIGURE 10—1 *Organizational chart*

PART-TIME TRIMMER (OPEN-HOUR WEEK)

The part-time person is someone who is going to school with a background in art or a related field. These people fill in evening hours and Saturdays. They are usually exposed to all phases of the display department and upon completion of school sometimes move into one of the areas of the department. They also work during the summer months for vacations and special displays. Whether they join the department or not, the working experience is a great help to them after they graduate.

BRANCH-STORE DESIGNERS (40-HOUR WEEK)

Branch-store designers' positions are almost the same as at State Street. They do get more involved in interior store trims. They also adapt State Street window trims to fit branch-store windows.

BRANCH-STORE FASHION PERSON (40-HOUR WEEK)

The branch-store fashion person works with the store managers in selecting window merchandise and then accessorizing it. He or she must spend time working with the State Street coordinator, learning new looks and accessory trends.

A TWO-WEEK SCHEDULE

The following are samples of listings of the merchandise for a two-week period. The window sheets go out to all departments for customer service in locating merchandise in windows. A diagram of windows also helps the sales personnel to locate specific merchandise in a particular window. The number of examples provided is to give an idea of the various window schedules.

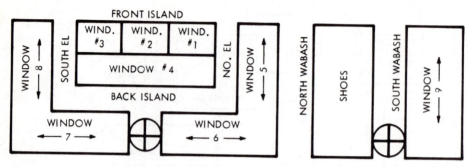

WINDOW SCHEDULE FOR TUESDAY MAY 25, 1971

STYLE & LINE	SIZE	DESCRIPTION	PRICE	
DEPT. 22		DESIGNERS		FRT. ISLAND
2146M/648	10	Blk. pants & skirt/prt. blouse	310.00	
DEPT. 34		ETIENNE		
516/7524	12	Blk/wht. lg. gingham dress/pants	68.00	
DEPT. 12		FARMINGTON		
596/356	10	Blk/wht. 2 pc. dress/red scarf	76.00	
DEPT. 15		JR. SPORTS		BACK ISLAND
1538/1222	M	Nvy/wht. striped top/solid skirt	20.00	
1538/1220	L	Nvy. knit shortall	19.00	
1538/2300	M	Lilac puffed sl midriff & short	25.00	
7603/645	S	White plaquet frt. antron top	11.00	
1399/7620	9	Purple velour shortall	13.00	
1538/033	S	Gold ribbed lg. sl. tunic	16.00	
DEPT. 21		JR. DRESSES		
6936/2404	7	Denim overall hot pant/orange bl.	28.00	
8252/8256	7	Tie dye hot pants/lace tie frt.	24.00	
7796/7305	9	Red/wht. arnel prt. dress	26.00	
367/1725	9	Wht. dress w/red/nvy trim/jkt.	34.00	
8190/3031	9	Purple/multi hot pants emb. frt.	28.00	
6382/1112	9	Water frt. scene cranberry pant/wrap	28.00	
1413/3861	9	Multi/blk prt. dress/tie waist	18.00	
5065/9008	9	Purple/nvy dress/Lanz	26.00	

FIGURE 10–2

STEP-BY-STEP TRIMMING OF A WINDOW

I. It is important everyone arrive on time each day, so as to be ready to start work promptly at 8:00 A.M. All merchandise and props should be removed and replaced between 8:00 A.M. and 9:00 A.M. so that no mannequins or large props have to be transported when customers are in the store.

II. Each person will carry props or transport mannequins to the window that is to be trimmed.

III. Actual trimming:

A. All accessory merchandise is removed from mannequins and niches.

1. Merchandise will consist of gloves, jewelry, scarves, flowers, hats, and so on.

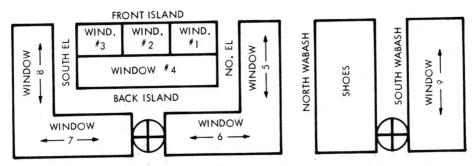

WINDOW SCHEDULE FOR WEDNESDAY MAY 26, 1971

STYLE & LINE	SIZE	DESCRIPTION	PRICE	
DEPT. 22		DESIGNERS		WIND. 5
647/776	10	Red/wht. check gingham midi/emb.	85.00	
6325/2838	10	Red/wht. check gingham midi wht. lace trim	90.00	
6448/354	8	Red prt. midi scoop neck/ribbon trim	130.00	
6448/425	10	Pink/grn. check gingham midi lg. sl.	165.00	
DEPT. 47		FARMINGTON		WIND. 6
5422/636	8	2 pc. green/wht. suit	30.00	
1298/241	M	Green voile cover-up	12.00	
5422/635	10	1 pc. green/wht. suit V neck	34.00	
5422/723	8	Blk/pink org. 2 pc. suit	20.00	
5422/722	10	Matching 1 pc. suit	30.00	
5422/741	S	Matching long pant	22.00	

FIGURE 10—3

2. Merchandise should be wrapped in tissue by departments and placed in boxes.
3. All wrapped accessories should then be placed in the accessory room to be counted back into stock by the Assistant Fashion Coordinator.

B. All mannequins are removed and returned to the display floor to be undressed later in the day.

C. All props are removed and returned to the display floor.

IV. Windows are now stripped and ready for retrimming.

A. All nails, staples, wire, and so on left from the last display will be removed.

B. New props are placed.

C. The mannequins (which have been predressed) are placed.

D. Mannequins are accessorized and finished by the mannequin dressers.

E. The floors are vacuumed.

F. The lights are checked and burned-out lamps are replaced.

G. The troughs next to the glass are cleaned with a damp cloth.

H. Signs are placed.

I. A final check of mannequins and props is made.

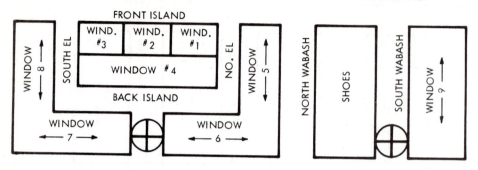

WINDOW SCHEDULE FOR THURSDAY MAY 27, 1971

STYLE & LINE	SIZE	DESCRIPTION	PRICE	
DEPT. 98		KNITS		WIND. 7
7047/3505	12	Nvy/wht. checked pant & skt. wht. blouse	70.00	
7047/1940	10	Nvy. sl. dress white stitching	38.00	
7047/1882	12	Red sl. dress white stitching	36.00	
DEPT. 17		STEPHANIE SHOP		WIND. 7
790/8768	12	Nvy/red/wht. stripe dress/solid jkt.	46.00	
4673/1627	8	Striped Culotte dress	32.00	
4673/2229	10	Red madras hot pants & wrap skt.	44.00	
4673/2420	12	Nvy/red/wht. blazer/wht. hot pants	48.00	
DEPT. 34		ETIENNE		WIND. 8
4456/1182	10	Seersucker lg. skt. hot pant	46.00	
7871/922	8	Pink gingham ck. skt. hot pant	75.00	
7871/917	12	Pink gingham ck. long dress	56.00	
9747/76711	8	Red/wht/bl. gingham dress ruff. hem	38.00	
9747/76639	10	Red/wht/bl. crop top	20.00	
9747/76184	10	Red/wht/bl. carioca skirt/ruffle trim	38.00	
516/7524	12	Blk/wht gingham dr./hot pant	68.00	

FIGURE 10−4

    V.   Mannequins from windows are undressed and the merchandise is returned to the department.

   VI.   Props from the previous window are returned to storage and new props are set up for the next day's trimming.

  VII.   Mannequins for the next day's window are dressed and made ready to be taken to the windows.[1]

DO'S AND DON'TS FOR VISUAL MERCHANDISERS

    1. Do not take price tags off merchandise.
       a. Manufacturers' tags may be removed.
       b. Price tags on accessories may be relocated.
    2. Never take tags, tickets, labels, etc., off furs. It is against the law.

[1]Provided by Chas. A. Stevens Co. of Chicago, Illinois.

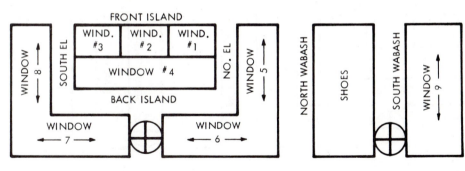

WINDOW SCHEDULE FOR FRIDAY MAY 28, 1971

STYLE & LINE	SIZE	DESCRIPTION	PRICE	
DEPT. 13		WABASH II		WIND. 9
7900/5450	10	2 pc. print arnel	32.00	
7900/5355	10	Polka dot culotte	32.00	
7900/5534	10	Polka dot Hot pant	32.00	
DEPT. 59/11		PATIO II		
5242/3044	12	Lime green dress/rick/rack trim	17.00	
8532/14206	10	Green/wht. hot pant dress w/floral		
		maxi skirt attached	28.00	
5242/3092	8	Lime green hot pants/maxi skt. att.	23.00	

FIGURE 10—5

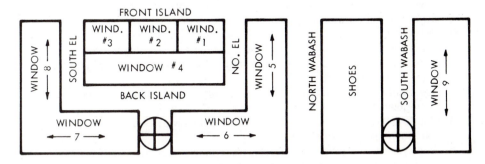

SUBWAY WINDOW — BUDGET COATS

STYLE & LINE	SIZE	DESCRIPTION	PRICE
DEPT. 70			
5562/2776	10	Navy Suit	21.00
5562/2770	10	Green sl. suit	21.00
5562/2772	10	Green suit/rounded coll.	21.00

FIGURE 10—6

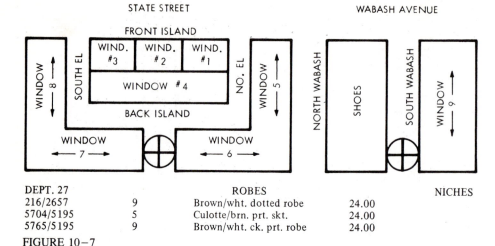

DEPT. 27		ROBES		NICHES
216/2657	9	Brown/wht. dotted robe	24.00	
5704/5195	5	Culotte/brn. prt. skt.	24.00	
5765/5195	9	Brown/wht. ck. prt. robe	24.00	

FIGURE 10−7

3. Do not stick pins in leather (handbags, belts, gloves, wallets, etc.).
4. Do not use masking tape on leather or suede.
   a. It pulls the nap off.
   b. It pulls the leather finish off.
5. Never put the store's gloves on mannequins, only gloves from the display department. Never put gloves on regular mannequin hands. (Use rubber or wooden glove hands only.)
6. Every piece of damaged merchandise is paid for by the visual merchandising department if it has been signed out to visual merchandising; therefore, try not to snag hose or scarves or step on gloves or jewelry.
7. Never put window keys in your pocket.
8. Never take keys out of the store.
9. Never go anywhere without letting your supervisor know where you are.
10. Never leave a window unlocked.
11. Never take props, such as screens, up or down an escalator.
12. When taking a merchandise mannequin call, never leave a nude mannequin in the window or on the floor. You must always have a pressed garment ready for replacement.
13. Never put a piece of unpressed merchandise in the window. This includes the regular trim as well as window calls.
14. Most island doors can be locked from the inside. Always lock the door when you are in the window alone.
15. When returning interior and window merchandise, always leave the merchandise in the buyer's office only. Have either the buyer, assistant buyer, or floor manager sign the window list.
16. Always get your merchandise return slip signed by one of the people above and return it to the accessory room. It is the only record of returned merchandise.
17. If for any reason you will be late or unable to come to work, report the fact.

SUGGESTED ACTIVITIES

1. Together with a group of at least five members, construct a display in a downtown store window. Functioning as a display team, elect a group director and write job descriptions for each member, establishing each member's goals and objectives in terms of the general display objectives of the group. Pay special attention to time organization and deadlines.
2. Interview at least four members of a store's display team. Compare their views on how their display team functions. Point out any conflicting views as well as similar views when reporting the results of the interview to the class.
3. Describe (sketch) in detail three windows that might be used to create a soft-goods, a hard-goods, and a combination window centering around the same general theme and appearing simultaneously. Strive for unity as well as variety in your ideas, and coordinate so that an overlying theme is apparent. (See theme suggestions at the end of Chapter 8.)
4. Make four theme or title signs using a lettering style and sign-making materials that will enhance the overall theme of the display. Strive for creativity in selecting a surface for the sign and the sign illustrations, borders, and mounting.

Project Ten (Part 1): Optional Display Construction

The purpose of this project is to individualize instruction so that, during the ensuing weeks, display students may concentrate on their own special area of interest and gain display experience and skill that will benefit them in their career choice.

Students, consulting with the instructor, will select from the listing below the type of display with which they wish to gain experience. Then, construction time and evaluation criteria (in addition to the usual element and principles analysis) will be determined through student-instructor conference.

Displays may be constructed in the school through use of its display lab, bulletin-board surfaces, display-case areas, or other central locations for displays. This display assignment may also be done in a retail store or commercial institution, according to student-instructor agreement.

After a display site has been agreed upon, it must be determined whether the message will be institutional or promotional and whether merchandise will be selected. Signs and showcards will be prepared, props assembled, and the display lighting considered.

The display is to be evaluated according to display principles as well as the special criteria agreed upon by the student and instructor. The display evaluation may take place as part of the class period if an in-school display area is used, or by appointment if an outside institution provides the display space. The time allowed for construction and evaluation will depend on the type of display and display area selected:

Case and counter displays

In-store P.O.P. displays

Closed-back window

Open-back window

Semiclosed-back window

Corner displays

Kiosks

Pinned display story (several such displays in an area with a central theme)

Hard-line store front

Soft-line store front

Industrial trade-show exhibit

Institutional window

Total boutique (classroom or actual small boutique)

Within the time specified, the student will select five different display problems from the list.

DISPLAY CONSTRUCTION CHECK LIST

1. Decide on merchandise to be displayed.   _____
2. Select display area.   _____
3. Fill in display sketch sheet.   _____
4. Lay out the showcard.   _____
5. Produce the showcard.   _____
6. Arrange to obtain merchandise (use Loan
   Sheet if necessary).   _____
7. Clean and prepare display area.   _____
8. Accumulate props.   _____
9. Put the display in the display area.   _____
10. Evaluate the display (use Evaluation Sheet).   _____
11. Return merchandise.   _____
12. Return props.   _____
13. Clean display area.   _____
14. File materials on display in project packet for use
    in final portfolio.   _____

SKETCH SHEET

Name _____

Name _____

Name _____

Sketch # _____

(Display Area #)

S K E T C H

Materials from Lab: _____ (Numbers)

_____ (Numbers)

_____ (Numbers)

Outside of lab materials: _____

Merchandise: _____

Showcard theme: (Actual words to appear on card)

_____

Signature of Instructor:

_____

DISPLAY EVALUATION SHEET

Criteria	Possible Points	Points	Comments
Subject—Its appropriateness in the store situation	10		
Neatness and preparation of the display area	5		
Message and total effect	5		

Elements:
  Props
  Shelf
  Lighting
  Showcard
  Merchandise
	10		

Organization and planning:
  Promptness
  Sketch
	5		

Principles:
  Emphasis
  Harmony
  Balance
  Rhythm
  Proportion
	10		

Color—Theme and execution	5		

MERCHANDISING/PROP LOAN SHEET

The Visual Merchandising class at _____ School is in the process of constructing displays as part of their class activities. The students will be able to practice the various visual merchandising principles, procedures, and techniques better if they have a variety of display projects. Therefore, please loan them the materials as explained in the attached Project Sheet.

The student has the responsibility of caring for, using, and returning all of the materials. However, please understand that they will be used in actual displays.

Thank you again for assisting the student in receiving a practical learning experience.

Sincerely,

_____
Instructor's Name

11

Common Errors in Display

Many display areas—exterior or interior, windows or showcases, tabletops or shadow boxes—could be improved by the avoidance of a few common and obvious errors that decrease their effectiveness. Some of the display errors that can be noted and sidestepped are described below.

TOO MUCH MERCHANDISE

As mentioned earlier, display areas have tended to be overcrowded for two reasons. Early in the history of display, before the true value of display space was realized, the "pitchfork" method of showing everything in the store created very crowded windows. As display space began to be considered valuable, merchants seemed to think, erroneously, that the more items they put in the display area at one time, the more beneficial this area became. Both these reasons lead to ineffective merchandise display.

There is no hard and fast rule on how much merchandise should appear in a display area. One guideline, however, concerns the price of the merchandise to be displayed. Because each display area is valuable and costs the store money for lighting, space not used for merchandise, fixtures, and so on, must be made to pay for itself. If an item costs several hundred dollars, it may very well be the only item in a space, as in the case of the designer dress in the window of an exclusive women's shop. The profit on this one item will easily make up the cost of the window display. In the window of the low-priced variety store, however, where most items are of low cost and yield a small percentage of profit per unit, more units and combinations of merchandise are presented at one time, because it will take several sales to pay for the display space.

Caution must be exercised that a window or an interior display area does not appear to be crammed with many similar items, does not have so many different items as to lose any selling message that it might have conveyed, and does not appear esthetically offensive to the viewer.

TOO LITTLE MERCHANDISE

On the other hand, bare or half-empty windows, interior racks, and cases can be just as bad.

The bare look makes a business establishment appear to be going out of business, or in other ways indicates to the customer that the establishment is less than prosperous. The usual reason for a lack of sufficient merchandise in a display is that the merchandise was sold out of the display area and not replaced. Also contributing to the bare look is lack of consideration about props, lights, and other elements that enhance the total appearance of the display. Poor planning of what merchandise is to be available for display during a certain period, or of a display of a certain type, may also cause an area to appear bare, particularly when the display is following a theme. This problem will present itself most frequently when merchandise is to be borrowed, as the desired items may not be available. If merchandise cannot be obtained for a display, the most reasonable solution is to change the dimensions of the display area, making it appear smaller in relation to the merchandise and props.

LACK OF AN UNDERLYING THEME

Whether a display is in a window or a store interior, part of a storewide promotional effort or an independent entity, it should have a strong message or underlying theme.

The viewer should be able to understand the idea presented by a display in a matter of seconds. Too often, merchandise is simply placed in a given space without a selling message or motif of any kind. At the opposite extreme is the situation in which too many ideas or themes are presented simultaneously, making each of them ineffective.

The importance of having a theme becomes even more apparent when several types of merchandise are combined in a display area. In this case, the effectiveness of the promotional display message is dependent on the strength of the theme. An example of this occurs when soft goods, wood carvings, toiletries, eating utensils, and so on are all displayed in the same space. A theme such as *Imports* or *Gifts from the Orient* can pull it all together. Many stores embark on great storewide themes and motifs by having foreign fairs and other central theme efforts.

TOO MANY PROPS

Just as there is no exact amount of merchandise that must appear in a display area, neither is there a given number of props that should accompany an item of merchandise or appear in a given area.

Props enhance the selling message. But a window or display area should not be so heavily propped as to disturb the selling message and confuse the customer. There should be no question in the viewer's mind what items in the area are for sale and what items are props. Salable items should be in full view, not hidden by props. The error of overpropping a display area is often more serious than using too few props. Some merchandise, such as a priceless antique dining set, may need few props to complete its message. Other merchandise, especially when grouped, needs propping to elevate it, direct the eye to it, and otherwise tell the customer about it. Always use props to enhance merchandise.

INAPPROPRIATE PROPS

The use of props that are not *merchandise-enhancing* is a common error. For instance, there is the danger of selecting a favorite display prop, such as an antiqued orange crate, and finding a use for it in almost every display, even, say, a lingerie display. Or the student of display or small-store owner may prop an area and then simply change the merchandise. This creates monotony, leading people to think that the area is never changed, and therefore, discouraging them from viewing. Props must be evaluated as to whether they are seasonal, masculine or feminine, rustic or modern; and whether they will appeal to the proper age and income groups, according to the merchandise they are to enhance.

Also, because props play an important part in presenting a theme clearly, they must be in harmony with the merchandise. Therefore, background props, although expensive, cannot be used effectively from season to season, even though merchandise may be changed. An example of this would be the lack of effectiveness of summer clothes against the red velvet and fireplace that accompany a Christmas display.

DISPLAYS CHANGED TOO SELDOM

There are several timetables for the changing of displays. Many interior displays are changed daily, because they are effective and merchandise sold directly from them

FIGURE 11–1 *A back-to-school window showing interesting and appropriate props accompanying major items of merchandise, formally balanced.*

Compliments of Chas. A. Stevens & Co.

must be replaced. Most large windows will be changed anywhere from twice a week to every other week, depending upon the season of the year and the extensiveness of a current store theme. An example of a window that might remain on display longer than usual would be a large department store's Christmas window.

One guideline for changing displays might be the consideration of the expense and extensiveness of the display effort. Special windows and internal promotions have a longer life. No set of props or group of merchandise should remain in an area until it literally collects dust and all possible viewers in the community have seen it several times. Frequently changed display areas present more merchandise, more messages, and more opportunities to purchase to the consuming public. Displays must be kept fresh.

DISPLAYS CHANGED TOO SLOWLY

The time that a display area is vacant (or covered) is time that it is not selling. The longer it takes to remove a display from an area, clean the area, and put in a new display, the more profits are reduced from that area.

Those working in the field of display must learn to plan a new layout so that all props, merchandise, signs, and lighting equipment are prepared and assembled before the old display is taken down or removed. Only then is the display area quickly cleaned and prepared, and the organized materials for the new display are put in place immediately.

Displays should be changed at the time when traffic in front of and in the store is at its lowest. This may entail late evening or early morning work. Peak customer traffic hours are to be avoided.

The greatest contributor to slow display changes, however, remains poor planning of materials, props, and merchandise for the new display.

NO DISPLAY BUDGET

A problem in display laboratories and store display departments is often the budget, as it is in many other instances. A display can avoid the low-budget look by a reduction in the use of obvious prop items like crepe paper or construction paper, or perishable items like grass, weeds, and other things from nature. Too many poster-board signs (used to fill up space) should also be avoided.

A low budget for the purchase of props in a store or a display laboratory could and should lead to ingenious use of merchandise and creative prop production. Good theme development without elaborate background materials is possible. Techniques such as using large bath towels hanging on a clothesline to back up a towel display, instead of trying to tile the back of a window, add to both motif and merchandise exposure without adding expense. Often, packing boxes with interesting wood textures, such as orange or fruit crates, may be antiqued and used as props, expecially for imports. Items of furniture are growing in popularity as display props and often can be purchased inexpensively or borrowed for the occasion.

FIGURE 11−2 *Full view of the main floor−Christmas trim. An example of a storewide promotional theme with a long life.*
Compliments of Chas. A. Stevens & Co.

LACK OF ATTENTION TO DETAIL

There is probably nothing less professional than a display that is not completed. Items often left unfinished include these:

Pins are not removed from garments or are allowed to show.

Dirt and dust are not removed from surfaces.

Glass is not clean.

Signs are not dry or complete, or have ink stains or soil on them.

Signs do not have borders.

Items that are flown or suspended are not secured to stay affixed to the ceiling and walls for the duration of the display.

Dummies or mannequins are not appropriately accessorized.

Tools are left in the display area.

Floor coverings are not cleaned.

Floodlights are not hidden from view.

The display area is not checked from all angles.

And it is worth repeating that nothing will destroy the selling message of a display like dirt.

ERRORS IN APPLYING THE PRINCIPLES OF DISPLAY

Many functional errors that can be observed in displays are concerned with application of the principles of design discussed earlier.

One error that might be noted has to do with the *point of emphasis*. Each display should have a point at which the viewer's eye can start easily. Often, a display either has no definite point of emphasis or it has the emphasis point in the wrong place, such as the upper right-hand corner.

Another error affecting the esthetics of a display is that of poor *balance*. A

Compliments of Chas. A. Stevens & Co.

FIGURE 11−3 *An accessory niche area using interesting props to tie small items together in informal balance.*

display that is neither formally nor informally balanced but merely too full on one side and empty on the other will decrease the effectiveness of the display.

A common error concerned with *rhythm* is observed when many objects, some of them quite small, are displayed in a single area and no attempt at continuous eye movement is made. These displays appear to be scattered and spotty, and a special effort must be made to tie them together visually.

An interesting error in display is observed where props and merchandise are not in *proportion* to each other, or when items in a display are not in proper proportion. A miniature usually should not be combined with something of real size. If a display is to be done in miniature, it should be done so throughout. Also, extremely large objects of real size can dwarf small objects of real size.

SPECIAL PROBLEMS OF INTERIOR DISPLAYS

Interior displays must be set up carefully, with traffic patterns in mind.

If, as in a supermarket, outsiders are allowed to display their company's point-of-purchase materials anywhere in the store, aisles get crowded, customer traffic becomes jammed, and the shopper experiences loss of time and inconvenience. The appearance of the store also suffers when it appears overcrowded. A display person or merchant must resist the temptation to use all display materials available regardless of space, quality, and timeliness of the materials.

SUMMARY

Common errors in display to avoid are these: too much merchandise, too little merchandise, the lack of an underlying theme, too many props, inappropriate props, displays that are changed too seldom, displays that are changed too slowly, a low-budget look, lack of attention to detail, errors in applying the principles of design, and confused customer traffic patterns owing to too many P.O.P. displays.

SUGGESTED ACTIVITIES

1. Evaluate four local store windows according to the effectiveness with which the common errors of display, described in this chapter, have been avoided. Use slides for class presentation. Include a discussion concerning which errors seem to be most difficult to avoid in these instances.
2. List and describe at least five low-budget props. Include detailed directions on how to create and use them. Have this list produced in quantity so that each class member may have a copy.
3. Using the errors of display discussed in the text, submit a written evaluation, or present an oral report, on how these errors either harmed or were carefully avoided in your classroom display this week. Emphasize the error that you had to try hardest to avoid.

Project Ten (Part 2): OPTIONAL DISPLAY CONSTRUCTION

The purpose of this project is to individualize instruction so that, during the ensuing five weeks, the display student may concentrate on his or her own special areas of interest and gain display experience and skill that will be of benefit in a career choice.

Students, consulting with the instructor, will select from the listing below the type of display with which they wish to gain experience. Then, construction time and evaluation criteria (in addition to the usual element and principle analysis) will be determined through student-instructor conference.

Displays may be constructed in the school through use of its display lab, bulletin-board surfaces, display-case areas, or other central locations for displays. This display assignment may also be done in a retail store or commercial institution, according to student-instructor agreement.

After a display site has been agreed upon, it must be determined whether the message will be institutional or promotional and whether merchandise will be selected. Signs and showcards will be prepared, props assembled, and the display lighting considered.

The display is to be evaluated according to display principles as well as the criteria agreed upon by the student and instructor. The display evaluation may take place as part of the class period if an in-school display area is used, or by appointment if an outside institution provides the display space. The time allowed for construction and evaluation will depend on the type of display and display area selected:

Case and counter displays

In-store P.O.P. displays

Closed-back window

Open-back window

Semiclosed-back window

Corner displays

Kiosks

Pinned display story (several such displays in an area with a central theme)

Hard-line store front

Soft-line store front

Industrial trade-show exhibit

Institutional window

Total boutique (classroom or actual small boutique)

Within five weeks, the student will select five different display problems from the list.

DISPLAY CONSTRUCTION CHECK LIST

1. Decide on merchandise to be displayed.   _____
2. Select display area.   _____
3. Fill in display sketch sheet.   _____
4. Lay out the showcard.   _____
5. Produce the showcard.   _____
6. Arrange to obtain merchandise (use Loan
   Sheet if necessary).   _____
7. Clean and prepare display area.   _____
8. Accumulate props.   _____
9. Put the display in the display area.
10. Evaluate the display (use Evaluation Sheet).   _____
11. Return merchandise.   _____
12. Return props.   _____
13. Clean display area.   _____
14. File materials on display in project packet for use
    in final portfolio.   _____

SKETCH SHEET

Name _____

Name _____

Name _____

Sketch # _____
(Display Area #)

S K E T C H

Materials from Lab: _____ (Numbers)

_____ (Numbers)

_____ (Numbers)

Outside of lab materials: _____

Merchandise: _____

Showcard theme: (Actual words to appear on card)

_____

Signature of Instructor:

_____

DISPLAY EVALUATION SHEET

Criteria	Possible Points	Points	Comments
Subject—Its appropriateness in the store situation	10		
Neatness and preparation of the display area	5		
Message and total effect	5		
Elements: Props Shelf Lighting Showcard Merchandise	10		
Organization and planning: Promptness Sketch	5		
Principles: Emphasis Harmony Balance Rhythm Proportion	10		
Color—Theme and execution	5		

MERCHANDISING/PROP LOAN SHEET

The Visual Merchandising class at _____ School is in the process of constructing displays as part of their class activities. The students will be able to practice the various visual merchandising principles, procedures, and techniques better if they have a variety of display projects. Therefore, please loan them the materials as explained in the attached Project Sheet.

The student has the responsibility of caring for, using, and returning all of the materials. However, please understand that they will be used in actual displays.

Thank you again for assisting the student in receiving a practical learning experience.

Sincerely,

_____
Instructor's Name

12

Visual Merchandising Areas

MARKETING

P.O.P (point-of-purchase) experts are forecasting that their expertise will be more in demand in the future—partly because of their winning ways as "tie breakers."

Point-of-purchase advertising has had an 8 percent annual growth in recent years, while most other segments of the advertising world have been through rough times. Howard Stumpf, president of the Point-of-Purchase Advertising Institute, Inc., says about 10 percent of the $20 billion spent annually for all types of advertising goes for displays located where the buyer makes his selection. He predicts billings will rise as self-service merchandising increases.

One recent survey of customers patronizing mass-merchandising establishments found that 30 percent had made unplanned purchases, opting for name brands 81 percent of the time. Half of those who made such purchases said the primary reason was that they "saw it displayed." Another 30 percent gave that as a secondary reason.

So when heavily advertised competing brands battle down to the wire, P.O.P experts say, their services and creations are often the "tie breakers" in the final decision.[1]

BOUTIQUES

One of the most significant happenings in the world of visual selling during the past two decades has been the advent of the boutique concept and the "boutique look." The original French definition of *boutique* is a small shop selling separates and accessories. Our current interpretation of *boutique* includes a concept of a specialty store, often out of the way, selling unusual and high-style, high-priced merchandise.

The meaning of the term has thus been extended to include many types of retail operation. Today, a boutique is nearly any small shop, whether it is located on Carnaby Street in London, the low-rent district of Manhattan, the quaint main street of an American midwestern town, or a part of a large department store with a small-shop look, such as Henri Bendel's Street of Shops in New York City.

Boutiques of today encourage the customer to browse. Large stores use special display techniques and special props to set aside a particular line of merchandise in order to achieve a boutique effect. Boutiques themselves use antique furniture and other unique props to provide that special kind of atmosphere apparently so pleasing to today's customer. Therefore, the term *boutique* has come to mean many things,

[1]Adapted from "Marketing," *Nation's Business,* January 1972, p.83

Courtesy of Gimbels Midwest, Inc., Milwaukee, Wis.

FIGURE 12–1 *An example of the boutique technique of visual merchandising.*

particularly a new kind of merchandising technique in today's marketplace, rather than simply a type of small store.

With the increase in customer dollars, several factors have created the need for a new look and new technique of merchandising and display: greater quantities of merchandise available; increased imports in soft goods, fashion areas, and hard lines; new and increasing awareness of changing fashions; and a huge new teenage market. A boutique may specialize in one merchandising line, such as junior dresses; one price line; one merchandise source, such as French imports; or one market, such as the children's market; or it may include several of these ideas.

The props in a boutique are an important consideration. Many items of furniture and antiques that are used to enhance merchandise in the boutique are themselves for sale. Great care must be exercised to accumulate props in accordance with the look of the merchandise, whether it is a look of imported goods, the Old West, American antique, or youth. The props must not overshadow the merchandise as salable items and turn the fashion store into an antique shop. However, we should note that usable furnishings are probably the most popular and important of the boutique display props.

Important features of boutiques, in addition to special merchandise and unique props, are the interesting permanent architectural details and intriguing graphics that frequently accompany them. Large spaces are divided into small, intimate areas. Special store fronts are used to set the small boutique apart from its often drab surroundings in an out-of-the-way location. In some instances, the merchant's creativity reaches outside the boutique, and the store front is painted, and its motif and color are changed with the change of the seasons and changes in the merchandise selection. Many boutiques are located in atmospheric brownstone houses or huge old frame houses.

SIGNS

Signs and a store signature are important. A special type of lettering may be used to represent the boutique and be carried through on bags, matchbooks, delivery trucks, and advertisements. The more unusual this type of art work is, the more effective it will be in distinguishing the independent small boutique from its competitors.

Whether boutiques are located as individual shops in a large store or exist as independent entities, they offer many unique experiences to the consumer. They permit easy accessibility to the merchandise, allowing the customer to touch and inspect it. They present individual attention from and contact with the salesperson; great product variety, if not great depth; and the opportunity to select uncommon items of merchandise. They are small enough, and often flexible enough, to provide the latest in fashion and social trends, so that they can easily hop on the bandwagon of the newest merchandising techniques and products.

Advantages that the boutique idea holds for the store owner include an answer to the merchandise/floor-space ratio, because the space may be fully filled with salable merchandise and props. The uncluttered look is not a necessity in boutique operations. In addition, boutiques provide an outlet for the most creative and current types of merchandising as they arise. They provide merchants and store managers with the opportunity to be creative with display techniques, because they are limited only by their imagination. And high-profit items and fashion trends may be merchandised effectively with great speed.

Among the problems resulting from the boutique idea is the cost of building and redecorating materials. This has been simplified by the introduction of new types of building stocks, so that any error of shop placement in a department store can be easily corrected. But the introduction of many boutique ideas in one store has caused some decision-making problems. Placement of a boutique in a department store can interrupt the optimum flow of customer traffic, if it has not been carefully planned.

Despite any possible problems, however, the boutique movement has many more advantages than disadvantages and is apt to survive for many years. It will probably be noted as one of retailing's most exciting changes.

THE BOUTIQUE ATMOSPHERE

Unique setting

Unusual and carefully selected merchandise

Small and intimate atmosphere

Excitement

Special help from sales personnel

Open display of merchandise

Customer involvement with merchandise

Small fixtures, lighting design, props, display color, and signs

Creative and imaginative decor

SUPERMARKET DISPLAY

Nowhere is good display more important to profits than in the American supermarket. Because supermarkets operate on such a small percentage of profit, it is imperative that all items appear as tempting as possible.

Props used in supermarkets are usually confined to shelves, racks, and merchandise pyramids and fixtures, which are provided by the total store decor. In displaying food items, two consideration are imperative: The first is *absolute cleanliness*. A pin or particle of dust might be overlooked in a fashion window, but dust is never overlooked on a food item. The second consideration is the *placement of the food items where they will be seen* by the customer. Many impulse items, for example, are placed next to the checkout stand so that they fall into the range of vision of the customer who is waiting to check out. Most food items are accessible to the customer, because food stores are generally self-service, and most are at eye level to provide for easy visual and physical accessibility. Also, the same product may be displayed at several points in the store, so that it is next to other items that it might accompany at a meal.

Signs are extremely important in supermarkets. Outside signs announcing specials are sometimes presented in almost a shorthand, understood only by the housewife who wants to know about as many sale items as possible for the weekend. These signs are often used against the front window and must be easily read, colorful, and informative. Interior signs included aisle information signs as well as special-sale signs.

Color is important in the supermarket, and bright, clear, clean colors prevail.

HARD-LINE DISPLAYS

Hard-line displays include merchandise that is nonflexible. Many of these items are small, such as those found in hardware stores—tools, light fixtures, paints, and so on. Also included in hard lines are many gift and accessory items that are small and need special fixturing and shelves to make them appear as a unit. Hard lines also include china, silver, glassware, pottery, and cookware for the home, along with dozens of home gift items. Each of these merchandise categories presents special display problems. Radiation, progression of sizes, and repetition of shapes are used to give these displays rhythm.

Props that are easily used to unify hard-line displays include shelves, counter tops, steps, and so forth, which help the items appear as display units.

If hard-line goods are large, like furniture and appliances, they require a setting, such as a room. They appear within the prop area rather than upon props. Appliance departments and stores, hardware stores, and hard-line gift areas have a tendency to appear spotty and cluttered if the goods are not displayed properly. This is due to the fact that many items must be visible to the customer simultaneously for a proper selection to be made.

DISPLAYS OF SOFT GOODS

Fashion merchandise falls under the heading of soft goods, which include men's, women's, and children's ready-to-wear, and linens, towels, and other home furnishings. These merchandise lines are easily draped and folded and lend themselves well to displays using continuous line eye movement as a method of creating rhythm in display.

Common props used in soft-goods displays include mannequins, T-stands, racks, pinned surfaces, and furniture fixtures. Displays may range from one-mannequin displays to those using mannequins, shelving fixtures, and other combinations of soft-goods props; and from single items where the merchandise is of substantial value to complete, accessoried units displaying many items, such as several coats accessoried by hats, boots, scarves, handbags, and jewelry.

One of the newest techniques of arranging soft goods of all types is to fly the merchandise, suspending it from walls and ceilings through the use of spool thread or other invisible wires so that it appears to be in motion. With this technique, fashion items can be shown in their entirety, without the use of mannequins and as they would be seen in motion. It is important never to fly merchandise in a way that contradicts natural body movement, such as bending forward at the knee.

Much is being done today with home furnishings like towels, sheets, and other linens. These are often put in a setting that implies their use in an appropriate room of the house. Bath towels would be seen with hampers, towel racks, soaps, wastebaskets, and even toilet seats of a corresponding pattern.

DISPLAYS USING MANNEQUINS

The use of mannequins in the display of apparel tells customers that fashionable merchandise is available to them and paints a picture of the garment on them. The display of mannequins creates a fashion atmosphere in the store, through fashion coordination, and helps to sell complete coordinated outfits.

FIGURE 12–2 *Mannequins are used to convey a family message–"Buy something for everyone for winter."*
Courtesy of Yosts.

Before the mannequin is assembled and dressed, it is necessary to have a display theme. Next, the clothing to be used must be selected and pressed. It must, of course, be fashionable merchandise. Accessories should be chosen carefully to complete the costume; often, the use of accessories will result in a total sale of all the merchandise in the display.

The next step is to select a background to create the proper atmosphere for the merchandise. It must enhance, not overshadow the merchandise or in any way present an opposing message. It is often a temptation to simply change the clothes on a mannequin, leaving in the same tired background week after week. The display then becomes out of season, as well as giving the passerby the impression that it has not been changed at all. The background provides the proper setting for the merchandise and should be considered each time the display is changed.

Mannequins are of different kinds: standing, kneeling, reclining, and action. There are mannequins with and without arms. Bust forms also may be used.

Most mannequins have "breaking points" at the shoulder, wrist, waist, and

FIGURE 12-3 *Display of soft goods—a fashion promotion for wash and wear with an ecology theme.*

thigh. Because the mannequin is not flexible like the human body, it is often necessary to "break" it at these points.

DRESSING A MANNEQUIN

When dressing a mannequin:

1. Start by covering the wig with a plastic bag to protect it.
2. Put on the lower half of the costume first, such as a skirt or slacks. When slacks are put on, the legs must be removed from the mannequin, inserted into the slacks, and fastened back onto the body. Then the clothing can be pulled up over the hips.
3. A shell or blouse is put onto the shoulders of a mannequin after the arms have been removed.
4. Some pinning of a garment is usually necessary. Use as few pins as possible, but make sure of a perfect fit. Be sure that the garment is pinned in the way the designer meant the lines to flow.

FIGURE 12–4 *An example of soft goods displayed, using the merchandise mannequins.*

Courtesy of Gimbels Midwest, Inc., Milwaukee, Wis.

5. The use of tissue paper may be desirable where more fullness is needed. This may be used to give a skirt a blown-out effect or to increase a bustline.
6. Check to see that the skirt hangs evenly and is well centered. To avoid having the hem show from the front, pin it higher in the back.

Change a mannequin as often as possible. Surveys show that customers return to shop every ten days. On each of their visits, show them something new to stimulate their interest.

FIGURE 12−5 *Front Christmas windows carry the same theme as the main floor.*
Compliments of Chas. A. Stevens & Co., Chicago, Illinois

SUGGESTED ACTIVITIES

1. Visit four boutique operations in your community and list the features of the windows you find to be unusual. Discuss how each provides reinforcement for the overall theme of the boutique. Submit a written report on your findings. Include snapshots if you wish.
2. Sketch or describe in detail how you would decorate and display a clothing boutique's exterior in order to set it apart from other store fronts surrounding it. Include comments on the role of the store front in merchandise display.
3. List all the considerations you feel make supermarket display effective. How is it different from other types of store display?
4. Using the same theme, the same props, and the same space or shelf, create a soft-line and then a hard-line display, changing only the merchandise, the lighting, and the arrangement of the merchandise according to display principles. Create these displays in class as a demonstration of the differences between soft-line and hard-line displays.

Compliments of Chas. A. Stevens & Co., Chicago, Illinois

FIGURE 12−6 *A sample of the type of mannequin in use at the present time. The price for a figure of this type starts at $235, but niceties such as glass eyes, portrait finish, and so on, run it over $300.*

EVALUATION

Essay

1. What are the three basic promotional policies a store may follow? Describe each of them. Which of these is the most common?
2. Name five possible themes for a store's displays.
3. What is the primary purpose of display?
4. Why is the work area of a display shop important to a display director?
5. "It isn't necessary for a display director to plan his displays in advance. He can always go out and purchase whatever he needs when he is ready to put in the display." Do you agree with this statement? Explain your answer.

True and False

1. For balance in a display window, an item that cost several hundred dollars should be balanced by adding two or three items of a low price. _____
2. A store display or window display should always have an underlying theme. _____
3. It is usually unnecessary to change displays more often than every three to four weeks. _____
4. Boutiques are unique shops that never caught on in merchandising. _____
5. Most boutiques encourage customers to touch and examine the merchandise. _____
6. Unfortunately, boutiques are unable to keep pace with the rapidly changing trends in fashion. _____
7. Most food stores today are self-service. _____

Project Ten (Part 3) : OPTIONAL DISPLAY CONSTRUCTION

The purpose of this project is to individualize instruction so that, during the ensuing five weeks, the display student may concentrate on his or her own special areas of interest and gain display experience and skill that will be of benefit in a career choice.

Individual students, consulting with the instructor, will select from the list below the type of display with which they wish to gain experience. Then construction time and evaluation criteria (in addition to the usual element and principle analysis) will be determined through student-instructor conference.

Displays may be constructed in the school through use of its display lab, bulletin-board surfaces, display-case areas, or other central locations for displays. This display assignment may also be done in a retail store or commercial institution, according to student-instructor agreement.

After a display site has been agreed upon, it must be determined whether the message will be institutional or promotional and whether merchandise will be selected. Signs and showcards will be prepared, props assembled, and the display lighting considered.

The display is to be evaluated according to display principles as well as the special criteria agreed upon by the student and instructor. The display evaluation may take place as part of the class period if an in-school display area is used, or by appointment if an outside institution provides the display space. The time allowed for construction and evaluation will depend on the type of display and display area selected:

Case and counter displays
In-store P.O.P. displays
Closed-back window

Open-back window

Semiclosed-back window

Corner displays

Kiosks

Pinned display story (several such displays in an area with a central theme)

Hard-line store front

Soft-line store front

Industrial trade-show exhibit

Institutional window

Total boutique (classroom or actual small boutique)

Within five weeks, the student will select five different display problems from the list.

DISPLAY CONSTRUCTION CHECK LIST

1. Decide on merchandise to be displayed.   _____
2. Select display area.   _____
3. Fill in display sketch sheet.   _____
4. Lay out the showcard.   _____
5. Produce the showcard.   _____
6. Arrange to obtain merchandise (use Loan
   Sheet if necessary).
7. Clean and prepare display area.   _____
8. Accumulate props.   _____
9. Put the display in the display area.   _____
10. Evaluate the display (use Evaluation Sheet).   _____
11. Return merchandise.   _____
12. Return props.   _____
13. Clean display area.   _____
14. File materials on display in project packet for use
    in final portfolio.   _____

SKETCH SHEET

Name _____

Name _____

Name _____

Sketch # _____

(Display Area #)

S K E T C H

Materials from Lab: _____ (Numbers)

_____ (Numbers)

_____ (Numbers)

Outside of lab materials: _____

Merchandise: _____

Showcard theme: (Actual words to appear on card)

_____

Signature of Instructor:

_____

Group # _____

Area _____

Name _____

Grade _____

DISPLAY EVALUATION SHEET

Criteria	Possible Points	Points	Comments
Subject—Its appropriateness in the store situation	10		
Neatness and preparation of the display area	5		
Message and total effect	5		
Elements: Props Shelf Lighting Showcard Merchandise	10		
Organization and planning: Promptness Sketch	5		
Principles: Emphasis Harmony Balance Rhythm Proportion	10		
Color—Theme and execution	5		

MERCHANDISING/PROP LOAN SHEET

The Visual Merchandising class at _____ School is in the process of constructing displays as part of their class activities. The students will be able to practice the various visual merchandising principles, procedures, and techniques better if they have a variety of display projects. Therefore, please loan them the materials as explained in the attached Project Sheet.

The student has the responsibility of caring for, using, and returning all of the materials. However, please understand that they will be used in actual displays.

Thank you again for assisting the student in receiving a practical learning experience.

Sincerely,

_____
Instructor's Name

13

Industrial Display

Institutions and companies producing and marketing industrial products use merchandise display in various ways. One type of display they prepare is known as an industrial trade-show exhibit. These exhibits vary in size and expense and are used in many situations to promote the company and its products. They may be set up at a manufacturer's show, such as a national machine-tool show, or they may be seen in the local junior high school as part of a career exhibit. A company may have more than one exhibit prepared to have the most appropriate one for a particular audience.

Manufacturers of both soft and hard goods use trade-show or trade-fair exhibits. They may appear as booths or may entail the use of an entire room or hotel suite. The exhibits may be product-oriented or institutional in the presentation of their message. This special type of industrial display is indeed an important aspect of industrial promotion and is a special challenge to the display creator.

There are several other patterns of displays used by industry. The following case is provided to give an example of industrial display in one corporation. It comes from a manufacturer of wrenches and mechanics' tools for industrial production and maintenance, and automotive test equipment and repair tools—the Snap-on Tools Corporation of Kenosha, Wisconsin.

Marketing more than 9,000 different products has presented many merchandising and display opportunities for Snap-on Tools Corporation over its half-century existence.

The tools are produced at seven manufacturing plants in the United States, Canada, and Mexico. Approximately 80% of the total sales volume is provided by more than 2,600 dealers and over 250 industrial salesmen, working out of 53 domestic sales offices. Additional volume is obtained through an international sales organization which blankets all areas of the free world.

The *Snap-on* dealer carries his tool stock in a walk-in van. This mobile operation permits him to bring his displayed stock of tools to all car dealers, service shops, service stations, and other tool users in his territory.

Snap-on Tools Corporation has three distinct markets that require specialized displays. The largest and most important area is the automotive mechanics that are serviced by independent *Snap-on* dealers with their walk-in vans. Second are the many industrial and educational representatives which are reached by *Snap-on* industrial salesmen as well as trade and school shows. Third, the foreign market is reached by distributors and trade shows. Each of these different markets requires vastly different display techniques.

In addition to the displays being designed for a particular market, there are many other objectives that each display must meet. The most important objective of any display is to help solve a merchandising problem. In fact, it is usually some sort of a problem that leads to the development of a display. As an example, let's examine the story behind the *Snap-on* screwdriver display.

Screwdrivers presented a merchandising problem for dealers. They needed a way to display them more effectively and in a very limited area. The display had to include all types and sizes of screwdrivers, in addition to multiples of each. And, in addition to creating point-of-purchase sales and simplifying inventory control of the units, the display had to be eye-catching, inexpensive, and rugged. All of the above problems became the design objectives of the display.

Basically, the following procedures are followed in the development of a display. First, a market and product research study is made in relation to each of them. In the case of the screwdriver display, this included determining which screwdrivers were the most popular and designing the display to hold these units in quantities justified for the most efficient inventory control. Second, the display is designed for functional use and the objectives that must be achieved. After a satisfactory sample has been made, it is field-tested, and the results evaluated. After a successful field test, prospective suppliers are given the opportunity to submit a price quotation for the job. A supplier is selected and production begins. Finally, the display is announced to the sales force.

If Snap-on Tools were to classify its displays as to usage, there would be four major divisions. First, the above-mentioned screwdriver display is a typical *dealer display* for point-of-purchase sales. Second, some displays are designed especially for *trade shows*– both domestic and foreign. On a much smaller scale are the more specialized displays designed for *international distributors* where tools are sold primarily in stores. And fourth, special *school display boards* are designed for educational programs.

Snap-on displays are true examples of the marketing concept. They are designed to do a specific job. They are not adapted to Snap-on, nor does Snap-on adapt to them, but rather each is developed to solve a merchandising problem.

Some of those problems, along with their solutions, were these:

1. *Snap-on Screwdriver Display*. The problems were: How to display screwdrivers most effectively including all types and sizes; how to display them in a limited area; how to create point of purchase sales; and how to simplify inventory control of the units. The display also had to be inexpensive and rugged.
2. *Flyer page announcing the display to the sales force*. Flyers are designed to give dealers an idea of what the display looks like, what it can do for them, and why they should have one.
3. *Hammer Display*. Although Snap-on had a hammer display available for dealer use, research revealed that a variety of hammer displays was needed to fill the display requirements of all their dealers. Each display offers a different approach to hammer display. See figures 13-1, 13-2, and 13-3.
4. *Snap-on sales promotion and business aids book*. To assist the sales force, a comprehensive and convenient book, listing and illustrating all props, business aids, and supplies was made up.

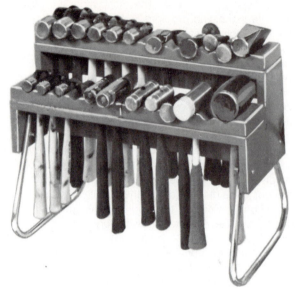

FIGURE 13—1 *Hammer Display. A variety of 24 hammers can be displayed with this handy two-level rack. Each slot is contoured to separate hammers. Legs and hardware included. Can be mounted to shelf or wall. Size: 24" wide and 7-¾" deep.*

FIGURE 13—2 *Hammer-Screwdriver Display. Attractively displays up to 24 hammers and 140 screwdrivers. Finished with natural wood stain, the display comes complete with all the hardware necessary for mounting. Size: 12"×30".*

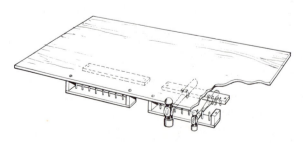

FIGURE 13—3 *Under-Shelf Hammer Display. Turn unused space in your van into display space with the under-shelf hammer display. An excellent sales aid in showing different types of hammer heads. Holds up to 18 hammers. Easily installs under van shelf.*

FIGURE 13−4

SUMMARY

Industrial display is practiced in a different setting from that of a retail store. However, the principles of display are the same. In every case, display people have a problem and must utilize all their knowledge, experience, and creativity in solving that problem. If they solve it successfully, they will meet the challenge to display and sell merchandise and image.

SUGGESTED ACTIVITIES

1. Class members may wish to form committees and obtain more information on industrial promotion by undertaking to:
   a. Visit local industry and, by appointment, interview industrial executives to determine the industrial promotion they use.
   b. Search through available magazines, texts, and other reference materials to determine how industrial promotion is implemented nationally and internationally.
2. If possible, visit an industrial trade show when one appears in your area. To gain insight into a trade show, contact a local industry representative and attempt to attend the show as a guest of that industry. If only one or two class members can attend, perhaps the class can choose them and be given a report on their return.

Project Ten (Part 4): OPTIONAL DISPLAY CONSTRUCTION

This project is intended to individualize instruction so that, during the ensuing five weeks, the display student may concentrate on his or her own special areas of interest and gain display experience and skill that will be of benefit in a career choice.

SPP-412A MULTI-WRENCH PROP

Some of the wrenches this prop demonstrates are: angle head, combination, Boxocket, flare-nut, ratcheting Boxocket, ratcheting open-end, spline and tappet open-end. Included with the prop are instructions for effective demonstrations.

BRUSH-ON PAINT
KRP-16A Red Lacquer (pint)
KRP-32A Red Lacquer (quart)

SS-638 POZIDRIV® "THERE'S A DIFFERENCE" CARD

Designed to be placed in your shirt pocket and passed out to your customers. This handout contains the information necessary for customer to distinguish between the Pozidriv® and Phillips® tip. The back of the handout contains the Pozidriv® story.

SPP-318A AIR TOOL DISPLAY

This sturdy and attractive black and white van display holds six air tools firmly on vinyl coated hooks. The following tools should be displayed on the board: PH50D, PH45A, IM3B, IM5B, FAR70B and PD3A.

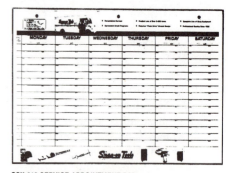

SSX-616 SERVICE APPOINTMENT PAD

This 60 sheet 18" x 25" pad provides your customer with space to write all service appointments. Backed with heavy-duty chipboard and three hole punched at top, it may be hung on a wall or used on a counter or desk top. Each sheet is perforated for removal and filing.

SS-649 LOCK ORDER GUIDE

A simplified guide for ordering the correct lock for a **Snap-on** tool storage unit.

PERSONALIZED MEMO PADS

Write your memos on personalized note paper. Two sizes of pads are available, 3" x 6" (50 sheets) and 5-1/2" x 8-1/2" (100 sheets). A red vinyl cover to keep the pad clean is also available. Red, black and white art decorates the top of each sheet and holder. These items can be ordered directly from the printer on the order form (SSX-672) which is available at the Branch.

FIGURE 13—5

144

Individual students, consulting with the instructor, will select from the listing below the type of display with which they wish to gain experience. Then, construction time and evaluation criteria (in addition to the usual element and principle analysis) will be determined through student-instructor conference.

Displays may be constructed in the school through use of its display lab, bulletin-board surfaces, display-case areas, or other central locations for displays. This display assignment may also be done in a retail store or commercial institution, according to student-instructor agreement.

After a display site has been agreed upon, it must be determined whether the message will be institutional or promotional and whether merchandise will be selected. Signs and showcards will be prepared, props assembled, and the display lighting considered.

The display is to be evaluated according to display principles as well as the special criteria agreed upon by the student and instructor. The display evaluation may take place as part of the class period if an in-school display area is used, or by appointment if an outside institution provides the display space. The time allowed for construction and for evaluation will depend on which type of display and display area are selected:

Case and counter displays

In-store P.O.P displays

Closed-back window

Open-back window

Semiclosed-back window

Corner displays

Kiosks

Pinned display story (several such displays in an area with a central theme)

Hard-line store front

Soft-line store front

Industrial trade-show exhibit

Institutional window

Total boutique (classroom or actual small boutique)

Within five weeks, the student will have selected five different display problems from the list.

DISPLAY CONSTRUCTION CHECK LIST

1. Decide on merchandise to be displayed.   _____
2. Select display area.   _____
3. Fill in display sketch sheet.   _____
4. Lay out the showcard.   _____
5. Produce the showcard.   _____
6. Arrange to obtain merchandise (use Loan
   Sheet if necessary).   _____
7. Clean and prepare display area.   _____
8. Accumulate props.   _____
9. Put the display in the display area.
10. Evaluate the display (use Evaluation Sheet).   _____
11. Return merchandise.   _____
12. Return props.   _____
13. Clean display area.   _____
14. File materials on display in project packet for use
    in final portfolio.   _____

SKETCH SHEET

Name _____

Name _____

Name _____

Sketch # _____

(Display Area #)

S K E T C H

Materials from Lab: _____ (Numbers)

_____ (Numbers)

_____ (Numbers)

Outside of lab materials: _____

Merchandise: _____

Showcard theme: (Actual words to appear on card)

_____

Signature of Instructor:

_____

DISPLAY EVALUATION SHEET

Criteria	Possible Points	Points	Comments
Subject—Its appropriateness in the store situation	10		
Neatness and preparation of the display area	5		
Message and total effect	5		
Elements: Props Shelf Lighting Showcard Merchandise	10		
Organization and planning: Promptness Sketch	5		
Principles: Emphasis Harmony Balance Rhythm Proportion	10		
Color—Theme and execution	5		

MERCHANDISING/PROP LOAN SHEET

The Visual Merchandising class at _____ School is in the process of constructing displays as part of their class activities. The students will be able to practice the various visual merchandising principles, procedures, and techniques better if they have a variety of display projects. Therefore, please loan them the materials as explained in the attached Project Sheet.

The student has the responsibility of caring for, using, and returning all of the materials. However, please understand that they will be used in actual displays.

Thank you again for assisting the student in receiving a practical learning experience.

Sincerely,

_____

Instructor's Name

14

The Visual Merchandising Team

OBSERVATIONS OF A VISUAL MERCHANDISING MAN

Editor's Note: Few outside the display field realize the depth of knowledge and know-how that the display director has—indeed, *must* have, to be effective in today's retail world. Al Coffey, display director of Whitehouse & Hardy, Roger Kent, and Frank Brothers, gave this talk at the First R.S.V.P. Seminar in June 1968:[1]

The biggest problem we have today and, I think, the most important is buying and promoting. The important thing in displays is buying to promote. Today you cannot take the chance of promoting for yourself, you have to have a promotion schedule. We do it on a six-month basis. We have key item lists on a six-month basis per month, and then we break it down into a four-week schedule. The people get their schedule on a four-week basis because this is the only way, we find, with all the fashion news around today, that we can possibly survive. You can't do it off the shelf—it's absolutely out of the question now. It's a rigid working schedule, but more interesting because you know in advance what you're going to do and can plan and create ahead. This is much more effective and the most important thing in men's wear today.

FASHION KNOWLEDGE IS IMPORTANT

The best friend that the display man has today is merchandising people—because you've got to work with them. You've got to understand their vocabulary—you've got to understand what it's all about. You can't wait until the winter's here to try to find out what the new fashions represent. You have to know well in advance in order to come out ahead of them.

Fashion awareness is something worth getting into now. It means we have to follow publications and read fashion magazines, just like the women have always done. We have to promote fashion news—everything is fashion today, and we find that the fashion merchandise is selling by far the best. The colored shirt, the wide tie—all news, and it's all selling so very well. Here in New York (I don't know how this relates to people outside of New York City), it's difficult to sell white shirts. Everyone wants a colored shirt; everyone wants a wider tie. Everyone wants a fancier tie. The fabrics of the ties are like kinds we have never seen—I have never seen. I have a wool tie on—I wouldn't wear a wool tie in the summer—but we're promoting this thing, and we've sold out on it. We don't have any left. . . .

[1]Al Coffey, "Observations of a Display Merchandising Man," *R.S.V.P.*, December 1968, pp.3–6.

NEED FOR AUTHORITY

Develop authority in men's wear—this is something we have never before done. Women's wear has always enjoyed authority. What they had in an editorial about the forthcoming season was authority. Whether you liked it or disliked it, you took it as authority. Men's wear has never enjoyed this until very recently. Therefore, what we put in the windows must be "authority." It must be well-planned, good-looking, and must help create the authority that women have always enjoyed. A good way to do this is, whenever possible, do an ad and a window together. When you have double emphasis, you're saying it in the window, and they see it in the paper and they relate to it in the window, or vice versa.

ATTITUDE IS IMPORTANT

The thing about "attitude"—people ask me very often about this awkward word—you have to develop an attitude about your store. Then people come to you and they assume that what you are saying is right. They accept the attitude of the store. We're working very hard on an attitude concept for the coming fall. We have to develop an attitude. We have to stand for something—and we must get the people who come to our store to say, "This is my store." A man with a store—and your store is his. . . . What is also important is for the salespeople to be "in" on what's happening—and to wear these latest styles. We have seminars for the salespeople—wine them, dine them, and make them feel a part of the company. We show them what's new, and our own people model these fashions, so that they become part of what's going on—even the people who just write out the sales checks. Everybody must understand what it's all about.

THE VISUAL MERCHANDISING DIRECTOR

One of the fundamental tasks of a store's visual merchandising director is the analysis of that store. The director must analyze the type of windows, interior display areas, and the overall layout of the retail facility, as well as considering such items as floor coverings, wall coverings, ceilings, and, of course, lighting.

Because much of the work of a visual merchandising director is performed in the display shop, this work area must be carefully planned and organized. The area should include an office, a large work table, a storage area, a painting space, and an area for the construction and creation of props, signs, and backgrounds.

The visual merchandising director must plan in advance all aspects of the store's display story if all merchandise and materials are to be ready when the display is to be constructed. Display materials assembled by the director might very well include woods, batting, seamless paper, wallboard, floor coverings, and a supply of appropriate power tools.

The visual merchandising director is seen as a store executive who must successfully combine people, processes, and ideas.

THE VISUAL MERCHANDISING DISPLAY TEAM

Regardless of the type of organizational structure an establishment has, all levels in the structure must perform as a team. Although many forces are at play deciding the team's effectiveness, each department can direct and control positive teamwork, gaining productivity through training and education. A program of training is essential. Included in the program should be general store policy, store operations, inter-departmental procedures, and specific skill application training in each area.

In any organization, each individual must be considered when establishing policies, training programs, and so on:

Organizational commitment refers to the nature of the relationship of the member to the system as a whole. Two general factors which influence the strength of a person's attachment to an organization are the rewards he has received from the organization and the experiences he has had to undergo to receive them. People become members

Courtesy of Gimbels Midwest, Inc., Milwaukee, Wis.

FIGURE 14—1 *The display is informally balanced. Props are used to frame the merchandise for ease of viewing.*

of formal organizations because they can attain objectives that they desire through their membership. If the person discovers that he cannot obtain the rewards he originally desired, either he leaves the organization and joins another, or, if this is not feasible, he accepts those rewards which he can obtain and, we suspect, at the same time feels less committed to that organization. On the other hand, obtaining the rewards sought operates to further his felt obligation to the organization, and his commitment is strengthened.[2]

Remember that rewards are not only monetary. They may be part of any total training program, and there are numerous ways to work toward obtaining a strong commitment from anyone in the store or a specific display department.

In summary, the effective utilization of human resources to achieve stated goals must be a top priority of any company.

A happy, committed team is a productive force.

TRAINING THE TEAM

The visual merchandising director should have a total training program for the department.[3] These questions should be considered:

Does each person have a job description?

Does each person know, understand, and implement the policies of the store and department?

Do you have a regular meeting with your personnel to discuss current important topics?

Do your personnel feel like a part of the department and organization?

Do your personnel know when they've done well or badly?

Do you have an orientation program for new employees in your department?

Do you have a continuous training program for all your personnel, and do they know its content?

Do your personnel understand how they are to be enlisted in the program, and by whom?

TYPES OF TRAINING

On or Off-the-job Training—Should the employee be trained on the job, and if so, during or after working hours? Should he or she be taken off the job and trained on company premises, or be sent away for training?

Formal or Informal Training—Should a training department be organized to train large numbers of employees on a formal basis, or should training be continuous and informal? Should there be a combination?

[2]Oscar Grusky, "Career Mobility and Organizational Commitment," *Administrative Science Quarterly,* 10 (March 1966), 488−503.

[3]Suggestion: The reader should consider studying supervision as a separate course.

Individual or Group Training—Should training be on an individual or a group basis? Should all employees be exposed to the same training, or should specific training be given to individuals and tailored to their specific needs?

Conducted by Company or Outsider—Should the company do its own training, or rely on an outside specialist? Should it be a combination of both?

Once the display director has analyzed the particular situtation and decided on the type of training program to be implemented, the specific type of training must be decided. There are various types of formal training that can be carried on within an organization. They can be classified thus:

Orientation—A new worker must be oriented to the tools of the job and the necessary information to make a satisfactory adjustment to the company, the department, the work group, and the specific job. Orientation training is usually the shared responsibility of the supervisor and the training department.

Basic Skills—When employees are hired or transferred to new jobs, they must be trained in the basic skills and procedures in order to perform the job at the level of proficiency the job and the company require.

Improved Efficiency—When a company changes a policy, plan, practice, or procedure, all members of the organization who are involved must be trained for the change. Whether concerned with safety, waste, or productivity, training of the employees will help them become more productive and safer.

Advanced Position—In recent years, many companies have assumed the responsibility of developing their employees for advanced positions. These programs are called supervisory, management, or executive-development programs.

Supervisor—Many supervisors are promoted from the ranks, and their previous training and experience have usually been focused more on *doing* than on *directing others to do*. The beginning supervisor needs many types of supervisory training to increase effectiveness in the new job. Training is usually in the realm of human relations, leadership, and basic principles of supervision.

DIRECTING THE TEAM

The visual merchandising director has now selected the overall training program, provided job descriptions for all the personnel, and implemented the plan, attempting at all times to utilize the human resources most effectively.

The question might be raised of how the display team functions within the director's plan. As an example, the Woodward & Lothrop Company operates within the concept of centralized display. The small suburban stores are grouped by twos and serviced by a "Roving Display Group Leader," who reports to the display director through the display manager.

All plans, schedules, and sketches are published in multiple copies and distributed to all supervisors. All stores follow the same plans, schedules, and sketches, and the production efforts of all are intended to have the same appearance, disciplined by the master plan of a centralized system.

The visual merchandising director visits each store as often as possible, especially if a need is evidenced. Each store is visited at least monthly, and a meeting in the director's office once a month brings all the display supervisors together with a preplanned agenda of forthcoming events. The notice of this meeting is sent out three weeks in advance.

After the monthly meeting in the director's office, the supervisors hold weekly meetings to further develop the ideas and plans with the members of their staffs and to activate the plans set forth at the director's meeting.

The display director is allocated funds at the beginning of the fiscal year. From these funds, the director and an assistant develop and administer the budget for display in all stores, including payroll, supplies, and minor categories. All budget information pertaining to any store is available to that store's manager, for that store only, for the purpose of containing the display department's budget within the structure of the store. The display director signs all purchase orders for the display department.

TEN COMMANDMENTS FOR DISPLAY PERSONNEL

A Chinese banker conceived these "ten commandments" for his employees. With some minor changes, these words of wisdom might have been written by a typical American manager.

1. Don't lie. It wastes my time and yours. I am sure to catch you in the end.
2. Watch your work and not the clock. A long day's work makes a long day short and a short day's work makes my face long.
3. Give me more than I expect, and I will pay you more than you expect. I can afford to increase your pay if you increase my profits.
4. Keep out of debt. You owe so much to yourself that you cannot afford to owe anybody else.
5. Dishonesty is never an accident.
6. Mind your own business, and in time you will have a business of your own to mind.
7. Don't do anything here that hurts your self-respect. The man who is capable of stealing for me is capable of stealing from me.
8. It's none of my business what you do at night, but if dissipation affects what you do the next day, you will last only half as long as you hope.
9. Don't tell me what I would like to hear, but what I ought to hear. I don't want a valet for my vanity, but for my money.
10. Don't kick if I kick. If you are worth correcting, you are worth keeping.

Although this might sound rather crude, it provides much food for thought. The display director, manager, or other employee can certainly interpret it in his or her own terms.

SUGGESTED ACTIVITIES

1. As a class project, create a total exhibit in the marketing department or marketing classroom area, promoting marketing programs and careers. (See boutique project in Chapter 12 and substitute a marketing theme.) Assign a display director to the total project and team directors to the various teams who will be creating displays in the areas under consideration. Use this total area display effort for an open house or a Christmas exhibit. Pay special attention to evaluating the total coordination effort. Have viewers cast ballots concerning their preference for one of the many display areas, thus evaluating display appeal.

2. Have a panel discussion including an industrial display director, a retail display director, a display supply-house representative, and a student of display. If professional directors are not available, students may prepare themselves to take these roles on the panel. Center the discussion around the functions of each of the directors and display team members. Get views from the panel on display as it exists today in our society and the role it will play in the future as competition increases in the marketplace.

Project Ten (Part 5): OPTIONAL DISPLAY CONSTRUCTION

The purpose of this project is to individualize instruction so that, during the ensuing five weeks, the display student may concentrate on his or her own special areas of interest and gain display experience and skill that will be of benefit in a career choice.

Individual students, consulting with the instructor, will select from the listing below, the type of display with which they wish to gain experience. Then, construction time and evaluation criteria (in addition to the usual element and principle analysis) will be determined through student-instructor conference.

Displays may be constructed in the school through use of its display lab, bulletin-board surfaces, display-case areas, or other central locations for displays. This display assignment may also be done in a retail store or commercial instituiton, according to student-instructor agreement.

After a display site has been agreed upon, it must be determined whether the message will be institutional or promotional and whether merchandise will be selected. Signs and showcards will be prepared, props assembled, and the display lighting considered.

The display is to be evaluated according to display principles as well as the special criteria agreed upon by the student and instructor. The display evaluation may take place as part of the class period if an in-school display area is used, or by appointment if an outside institution provides the display space. The time allowed for construction and for evaluation will depend on which display and display area are selected:

Case and counter displays
In-store P.O.P. displays

Closed-back window

Open-back window

Semiclosed-back window

Corner displays

Kiosks

Pinned display story (several such displays in an area with a central theme)

Hard-line store front

Soft-line store front

Industrial trade-show exhibit

Institutional window

Total boutique (classroom or actual small boutique)

Within five weeks, the student will have selected five different display problems from the list.

DISPLAY CONSTRUCTION CHECK LIST

1. Decide on merchandise to be displayed.   _____
2. Select display area.   _____
3. Fill in display sketch sheet.   _____
4. Lay out the showcard.   _____
5. Produce the showcard.   _____
6. Arrange to obtain merchandise (use Loan
   Sheet if necessary).   _____
7. Clean and prepare display area.   _____
8. Accumulate props.   _____
9. Put the display in the display area.
10. Evaluate the display (use Evaluation Sheet).   _____
11. Return merchandise.   _____
12. Return props.   _____
13. Clean display area.   _____
14. File materials on display in project packet for use
    in final portfolio.   _____

SKETCH SHEET

Name _____

Name _____

Name _____

Sketch # _____

(Display Area #)

S K E T C H

Materials from Lab: _____ (Numbers)

_____ (Numbers)

_____ (Numbers)

Outside of lab materials: _____

Merchandise: _____

Showcard theme: (Actual words to appear on card)

_____

Signature of Instructor:

_____

DISPLAY EVALUATION SHEET

Criteria	Possible Points	Points	Comments
Subject—Its appropriateness in the store situation	10		
Neatness and preparation of the display area	5		
Message and total effect	5		
Elements: Props Shelf Lighting Showcard Merchandise	10		
Organization and planning: Promptness Sketch	5		
Principles: Emphasis Harmony Balance Rhythm Proportion	10		
Color—Theme and execution	5		

MERCHANDISING/PROP LOAN SHEET

The Visual Merchandising class at _____ School is in the process of constructing displays as part of their class activities. The students will be able to practice the various visual merchandising principles, procedures, and techniques better if they have a variety of display projects. Therefore, please loan them the materials as explained in the attached Project Sheet.

The student has the responsibility of caring for, using, and returning all of the materials. However, please understand that they will be used in actual displays.

Thank you again for assisting the student in receiving a practical learning experience.

Sincerely,

_____
Instructor's Name

15

Visual Merchandising Trends and Practices

Customers react to displays in terms of the display appeal, overall appearance, and impact. Stores want customers to feel that the displays are made expressly for them, as is brought out in this poem:

GOOD BUSINESS — 1912
by Edgar Guest

If I possessed a shop or store
    I'd drive the grouchers off my floor
I'd never keep a boy or clerk
    With mental tooth-ache at his work
Or allow the man who takes my pay
    Drive customers of mine away.

I'd treat the man who takes my time
    And spends a nickel or a dime
With courtesy, and make him feel
    That I was glad to close the deal
For tomorrow who can tell,
    He may want things I have to sell.

The reason people pass one door
    To patronize another store
Is not because the busier place
    Has better gloves or silks or lace
Or cheaper prices, but it lies
    In friendly words and smiling eyes.

The only reason I believe
    Is in the treatment folks receive.[1]

The purpose of this chapter is to provide the reader with practical applications of visual merchandising in today's business world.

There are new trends and practices in visual merchandising today, found in both

[1]From Edgar A. Guest, *Today and Tomorrow,* by permission of the publisher, Reilly & Lee, subsidiary of Henry Regnery Company.

retail and manufacturing operations. Of the many forms and formats they take, this chapter will give two actual examples, demonstrating the integration of visual merchandising into store planning, merchandising, and so on, in a retail department store and in a manufacturing setting.

RETAIL DEPARTMENT STORE

VISUAL MERCHANDISING AS A TOTAL CONCEPT

More and more, visual merchandising is integrated with the total planning and operation of the store. Top-level executives such as the store planning director and the visual merchandising director meet with the top corporate executives of a company to determine such things as the corporate image, physical facilities changes, seasonal and fashion trend projections, and various other retailing innovations. Their decisions are reflected in physical store change procedures, as shown in the requisition in Figure 15-1.

Today, visual merchandising is definitely tied to store policy. No longer is the "window trimmer" a smocked, custodial, in-store employee. The visual merchandising executive visits the New York fashion market as well as other important markets. There, the executive consults with fashion buyers and visits many display fixture vendors, making purchases to update the visual merchandising techniques used for a store and a season.

Visual merchandising executives agree that the primary purpose of visual merchandising is to sell the merchandise, thus making the coordination, imperative at every level, between merchandise purchased and merchandise displayed.

MERCHANDISING AND VISUAL MERCHANDISING

Actually purchasing merchandise for a store to sell to the customer and presenting that merchandise to the customer in such a way as to make it appealing is and must be a two-way communication process if it is to be effective.

Buyers and visual merchandising executives often share opinions as to what will tell the story about what is "hot" in the market for the coming season. In the fashion area, the buyers ultimately make most of the decisions concerning purchases, but the visual merchandising people are in on these decisions all the way.

In the hard-line areas, visual merchandisers actually make decisions as to what could be purchased for a special promotion and/or visual presentation. In any case, the executives in charge of displaying a store's merchandise are no longer seeing the merchandise for the first time as it arrives in the store.

The visual merchandising department works with different departments in different ways, as we stated previously. It also does varying amounts of planning for different kinds of promotions. When it is important for the total store to present a unified theme, such as a holiday theme, the visual merchandising executives do up to 90 percent of the planning and ask each store's visual merchandising manager to carry

```
                              REQUISITION
_____

              STORE PLANNING – VISUAL MERCHANDISING
                      GIMBELS MIDWEST, INC.
_____


LOCATION          Store_____ Level _____ Dept. _____

CATEGORY          ☐ Fixturing/Hardware      ☐ Painting/Decor

                  ☐ Department Move         ☐ Department Renovation

                  ☐ Non-Selling             ☐ Other (New Dept. Promotion
                                               Seasonal Dept., etc.)


DESCRIPTION



REASON/COMMENTS


COMPLETION
DATE REQUESTED _____ INITIATED BY _____ DATE _____
_____


REVIEWED BY _____
           Visual Merchandising Director – Store Planning Director

COMMENTS                                     DATE _____

_____

DISPOSITION ☐ Approved    ☐ Not Approved    ☐ Review at Later Date _____
                                                                    V.P.

        APPROVED BY _____ DATE _____
                   Vice President

_____

CHARGE TO  CBR NO._____ EXPENSE NO._____
```

FIGURE 15–1 *An example of visual merchandising and store planning working together.*
Courtesy of Gimbel's Midwest, Inc., Milwaukee, Wis.

FIGURE 15–2 *Visual merchandising and store planning work together to produce effective displays.*

Courtesy of Gimbels Midwest, Inc., Milwaukee, Wis.

out the plans. During other times of the year, promotions are executed almost entirely by the visual merchandising managers in the branch stores, and a great deal of interpretive freedom is given to them. This system will vary, of course, with any one department store's organizational structure.

VISUAL MERCHANDISING ORGANIZATION

There are almost as many store organizational structures as there are stores, and the structure of a visual merchandising department will vary with the total store structure. One large Midwest department store is organized somewhat as in Figure 15-5.

A sample job description for a visual merchandising manager will show the manager's involvement with other areas in regard to teamwork emphasis:

1. Act as liaison between the central visual staff and branch-store personnel on presentation and problems.
2. Interpret and act on visual presentation problems within the manager's own store.
3. Relate any visual problem to the central visual merchandising department.
4. Train staff and store personnel on a daily basis in new techniques.

VISUAL MERCHANDISING DIVISION
SEASONAL SHOP REQUEST

DATE _____ DEPARTMENT _____ DIVISION _____

SPRING/FALL SHOP _____ HOLIDAY SHOP _____

CONCEPT:
    PERTINENT INFORMATION ABOUT MERCHANDISE (ATTACH STOCK ASSORTMENT) _____

_____

_____

_____

SPECIAL FIXTURING REQUIREMENTS (HANGING SHELVES, TABLES, MANNEQUINS, SIGNING, ETC.) _____

_____

_____

_____

SUGGESTED INSTALLATION DATE _____ PEAK STOCK LEVEL _____ TERMINATION DATE _____

PROJECTED SALES VOLUME 6 MONTHS _____ ADVERTISING EFFORT _____ INITIAL AD DATE _____

VENDOR COOPERATION _____

STORES	UNITS	DOLLARS INVESTMENT	DATE OF ARRIVAL	STORES	UNITS	DOLLARS INVESTMENT	DATE OF ARRIVAL
DT				SG			
MF				CC			
NR				AP			
SR				ET			
HD				MC			
				PP			

APPROVAL: DIRECTOR OF STORES _____ DMM _____ GMM _____

BUDGET ALLOTMENT:

        VISUAL MERCHANDISING _____ SIGNATURE _____

        STORE PLANNING _____ SIGNATURE _____

            TOTAL _____ DATE _____

FIGURE 15-3 *Another example of store forms, indicating the level of involvement of various positions in the organization and the integration of visual merchandising and store planning.*
Courtesy of Gimbel's Midwest, Inc., Milwaukee, Wis.

5. Work daily with store managers on store problems.
6. Be responsible for calling visual problems to the attention of the general manager—for example, merchandise out of class, racks out of alignment, dirty fixtures, or poor lighting.
7. Communicate with the fashion office on trend problems.
8. Teach visual theory to the visual staff in detail.

Courtesy of Gimbel's Midwest, Inc., Milwaukee, Wis.

FIGURE 15–4 *Effective visual merchandising calls upon all sources in store to work together.*

9. Teach display techniques to staff: design elements, planning, execution, fashion trends.
10. Follow store policies and monitor staff on them.
11. Interview personnel for staff vacancies.
12. Monitor and approve general fixture use and vendor fixtures.

The career path often followed to allow promotional movement in the organization and the background that has proved to be most effective are as follows:

1. Experience in retail selling
2. Experience in retail window trimming

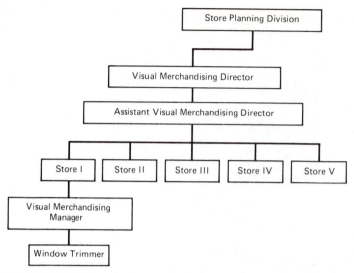

FIGURE 15—5 *Organization structure of a visual merchandising department.*

3. Technical college display courses where several displays have been executed.

There is simply no effective way to learn how to present merchandise to the customer without gaining experience in both handling the merchandise and relating to the customer.

Once a position has been obtained as a trimmer in a "flagship" store or a suburban store, upward mobility on the organization chart follows as positions open and as experience is gained. Any formal training usually involves a two- or three-day session in visual merchandising if the trainee is in the executive training program, but training is more frequently accomplished on the job, where the new trimmer works with one or more experienced trimmers.

The visual merchandising director is a sort of cheerleader, unifying the efforts of the store's fashion director or coordinator, the director's own visual merchandising team, and the store's salespeople, who must understand store promotional efforts if they are to sell to the consumer with enthusiasm.

Visual merchandising is becoming more and more important in giving a store a competitive edge, since many stores share merchandise sources and, therefore, carry many similar items. The thing that makes the difference is how the merchandise is presented. In other words, good visual merchandising gives the merchant an invaluable competitive edge as well as defining a store's personality in today's marketplace.

The quality of this visual merchandising is dependent on two major factors, according to Richard Sukolwicki and Linda Higgins, visual merchandising executives of Gimbel's Midwest: communications and flexibility.

Communications must allow for the free flow of information from the top corporate executives down through the window trimmers in each suburban store, as well as across the organization throughout the merchandising and operations divisions.

Flexibility comes into play when merchandise shipments are lost or delayed, props are not delivered on time, or major changes in plans need to be made in a considered theme because of new developments in the market, a political or social event, or a new merchandising method.

Again, visual merchandising may be the factor that becomes the most important in the competitive retail world of tomorrow.

The following checklist should be used by the visual merchandising staff prior to the daily store opening:

A. *All merchandise-related displays:*
  1. Are they intact?
  2. Clean, fashionably correct?
  3. Enough merchandise to support the display?
  4. Is the merchandise located on adjacent fixturing?
  5. Are presentations adequately lit?
B. Nonmerchandise displays
  1. Plants clean and healthy?
  2. Pictures hung straight?
  3. Ledges clear of litter?
C. *Fashion forward presentation*
  1. Is there stock to support fashion forward?
  2. Platforms clean, mannequins undamaged?
  3. T-stands layered neatly?
  4. Accessory items signed on loan still intact?
D. *Signing*
  1. Are signs and toppers removed after a sale event?
  2. Are remaining signs in good condition?
  3. Sign holders readable from both sides?
  4. Proper sign holders being used?
  5. No taped signs?

MANUFACTURING

The following description of a visual merchandising program was set forth by Jockey International, Inc.

INTRODUCTION

Jockey for over the past 100 years has led the industry in merchandising men's underwear with innovative ideas and techniques.

Jockey was the first to develop:

—Self-selection fixturing

—Packaged men's underwear

VISUAL MERCHANDISE STORE VISIT REPORT

STORE: _____

DATE: _____

SIGNED: _____

STORE MANAGER: _____

V.M. MANAGER: _____

	EXCELLENT	GOOD	FAIR	POOR	COMMENTS
COLORING OF MERCHANDISÉ					
MANNEQUIN PRESENTATION					
FRONT & FORWARD PRESENTATION					
CORRECT USE OF FIXTURES					
CORRECT PLACEMENT OF FIXTURES					
SIGNING (STORE & VENDOR)					
COUNTER FIXTURES					
CASE DISPLAYS					
TABLE PRESENTATIONS					
LEDGE APPEARANCE					
FURNITURE FLOOR					
MODEL ROOMS					
GENERAL APPEARANCE					
WINDOWS					
V.M. SHOP CLEANLINESS ORGANIZED					
FOLLOW THROUGH OF PROMOTIONAL EFFORT					

COMMENTS

FIGURE 15—6 *An example of a visual merchandise evaluation form used by store managers and visual merchandising managers.*

Courtesy of Gimbel's Midwest, Inc., Milwaukee, Wis.

—Lifelike mannequins for display

—The brief garment

—A full line of fashion underwear

As the fashion underwear business becomes more and more important, the need to adequately display and properly merchandise this category takes on an added dimension. Creative packaging has proven significantly important in selling fashion underwear and the need for a universal display/merchandising device is paramount.

The need to further update in-store merchandising is evident. Concept 80's meets that marketing planning and design need.

THE CHANGING MARKET

Retailing has changed dramatically in recent years. Society's lifestyles have shifted to a more casual atmosphere.

Today's cultural/social influences have caused store design to supplement

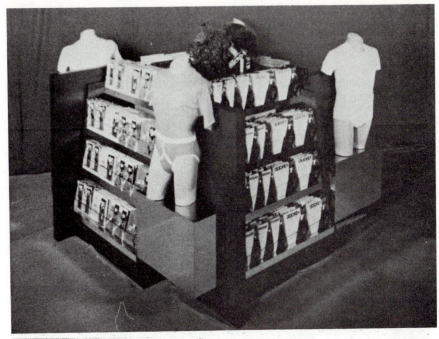

FIGURE 15–7 *Example of visual merchandising and store planning assistance provided by a merchandise manufacturer.*

Courtesy of Jockey International, Inc., Kenosha, Wis.

merchandise. Aisles meandering through the store move customers to all areas using fixturing, ceiling structure, and a variety of floor surfaces. The traditional island counters with straight structured aisles have given way to a self-service approach.

Jockey merchandising programs have paralleled the cultural/social changes that have taken place in the retail design.

Fashion bikinis and briefs are the fastest-growing items in the men's underwear market. These categories experienced total market share increases of 16.6% and 5% for the twelve months ending in June 1979.[2] *(Jockey brand bikini-type brief sales are up 69% for the first six months in '79.)*

OBJECTIVE

Develop a program for housing, display, merchandising, and identification of fashion underwear.

Develop a program on the importance of Jockey brand underwear relative to its performance, profitability, and return on investment to the retail store.

Pfeiffer and Miro Associates, New York, were commissioned to assist in the coordination of this study. Recognized as leaders in the field of retail planning and design, we drew upon their 20 years' experience, knowledge, and expertise in the retail

[2]Source NPD Research, Inc.

business. They have served major department and men's specialty stores from coast to coast.

The findings and conclusions reached are from actual case studies, on-location observations, conferences, and surveys taken from over 100 top department and retail stores.

Tomorrow's opportunities are here today as Jockey extends its professional guidance, in the location, appearance, function, and fixturing of the men's underwear department as partners planning for profit.

RETAIL PLANNING

Today's customer is a sophisticated shopper extremely conscious of trends that influence his or her lifestyle and buying habits and have made a strong impact on total store merchandising. Informality and naturalness in the store appearance and merchandising are a direct response to customer attitudes.

Men's wear, furnishings, and especially underwear departments are one of the major growth areas in department stores. It is indeed a very new phenomenon to locate men's underwear in a prominent location on an easily accessible traffic aisle. With visual merchandising directions beginning to have an interest in the display of personal furnishings, a very healthy maturing of attitudes is at hand.

Innovative planning, the design of the area, the modular fixturing, and the lighting all contribute to the proper merchandise presentation.

The following studies [Figures 15-8 and 15-9] indicate several vital factors. In order for underwear, Jockey brand, to continue a growth pattern within a department store environment, regardless of store volume, locations must be improved. High-

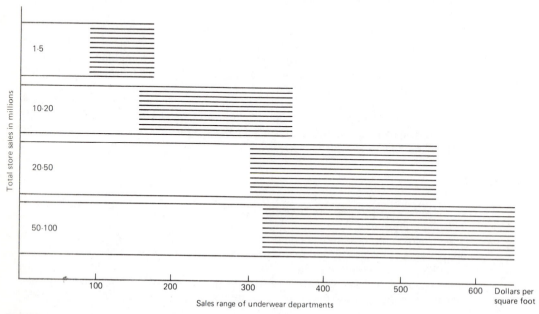

FIGURE 15−8 *The chart illustrates in dollars per square feet the cross-section findings of what approximately 100 department stores of various dollar volumes and locations of men's underwear departments contribute to the total store.*

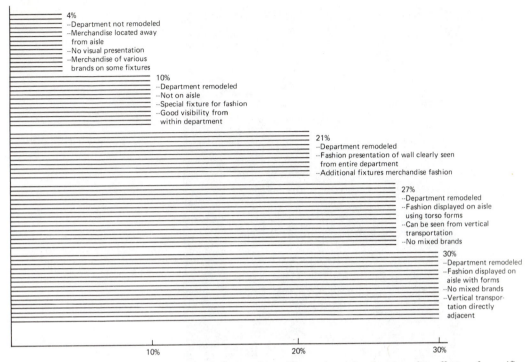

FIGURE 15-9 *Graph illustrates the findings of an 18-month study showing the effects of specific merchandising design and planning which contribute to the volume influencing underwear sales . . . dollars/square foot.*

fashion underwear must be visible and accessible. The visual presentation must support the high-fashion underwear and encourage total wardrobe coordination.

COMPONENTS

Contemporary, functional, maximum capacity and display to complement and highlight the decor of a men's underwear or furnishings department.

Basic and fashion basic merchandise housing in patented Jockey Dispens-o-matic units in singular or modular groupings. Capacity and display are paramount.

The high-fashion pyramid is designed and stepped vertically for sizing. Chrome, wood, and plexiglas compliment any decor. Visual display of patterns and colors.

The pyramid on platform base with plexiglas envelop display. Torso and poster displays excellently relate high fashion with product in use.

A lighted superstructure to highlight merchandise presentation.

CONCEPTS

Principles of internal arrangements of Jockey underwear departments.

—Arrangements today are "natural." . . . Customers are encouraged to browse and walk around fixtures, providing good exposure of every merchandise category.

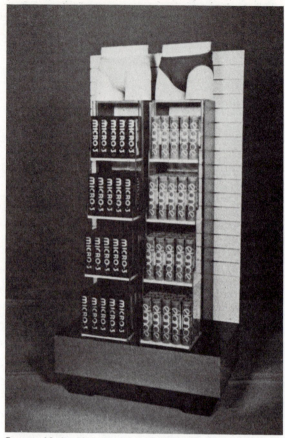

Courtesy of Jockey International, Inc., Kenosha, Wis.

FIGURE 15–10 *Jockey was the first to develop self-selection featuring packaged men's underwear.*

—High-impact, impulsive fashion underwear requires prominent, up-front traffic locations.

—Display and graphics are vital components to the merchandise and desirable to coordinate underwear selections and colors to the total men's wardrobe.

—Jockey underwear is entirely packaged merchandise. Instant relation to a visible garment on a torso is essential to the organization of underwear in fixtures and unconfused selection by the customer, thus reducing package tampering.

—Fashion underwear should showcase the department, be readily seen and accessible from anywhere within the underwear or furnishings department, traffic aisles, or vertical transportation.

The following are plans, designs, and elements that suggest ideas contributing to a successful, efficient, definitive Jockey brand underwear department.

—Flexible in size and shape of the area

—Use and appearance of walls to support department

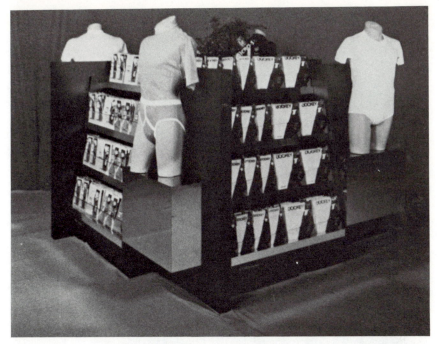

FIGURE 15–11 *Basic and fashion merchandise housing and patented jockey dispensers—O-Matic unit in singular or modular groups.*
Courtesy of Jockey International, Inc., Kenosha, Wis.

—Fixture types and density in use for a complete underwear department
—Appropriate use of signing and Jockey logotype for department identification
—Colors and materials that complement, not conflict with, the merchandise
—Complementary displays and graphics to emphasize the fashion significance of underwear

These all contribute to improved net profits. Improved Jockey underwear departments depend on a close coordination between merchandising, store planning, visual merchandising, and Jockey International. We then become partners in planning for profit.

PLUS—JOCKEY PROVIDES:

Superior Service
Productive Fixturing and Display
Complete Merchandise Programs
Attractive Packaging
Strong National and Local Advertising
Inventory Management

FIGURE 15–12 *Jockey's successful pyramid display unit uses a combination of packaged merchandise, mannequins, and props.*

Courtesy of Jockey International, Inc., Kenosha, Wis.

Project Eleven: DISPLAY CONSTRUCTION IN TOTAL STORE INTERIOR WITH STUDENT EVALUATION OF ALL DISPLAYS

This project is intended to give all students an in-store experience, with realistic time limitations, wide merchandise selection alternatives, and display-team cooperation.

The instructor will arrange for either half the group or all of it to assemble at a retail store during slow traffic hours or when the store is closed. This may be done with half the group on two different days, or, if the store has enough display areas, it may include the entire class on one day. As the students arrive at the store at the appointed time, the instructor will assign one of the display areas of the store to each person or team, as the project. These areas may include hanging displays, front windows, cases, counters, table surfaces, mannequins, kiosks. Windows will be done by display teams; all other areas will be tackled individually.

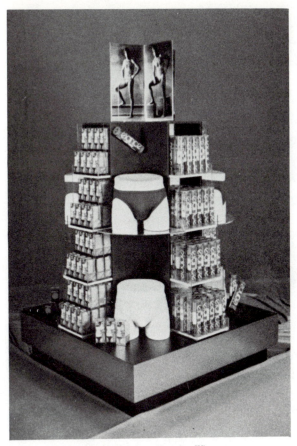

FIGURE 15–13 *The high fash-*
ion pyramid is designed and
stepped vertically for sizing.

Courtesy of Jockey International, Inc., Kenosha, Wisc.

The student will be able to select merchandise from the stock in the store after brief consultation with the attending store consultant and after consultation with other class members to avoid duplications in displaying merchandise. The props provided by the store will be used. Available store signs will be used, and previously lettered signs of professional quality, which the student might wish to have prepared as general statement signs, can be incorporated. Only store lighting facilities will be used.

The display effort in the store should be terminated after one and a half hours. Evaluation will be handled by appointment. The person putting in the display, the instructor, and the store consultant will confer in reference to the display. Because the store will have agreed to retain the displays for at least three days, appointments may be made within this time.

After the display is evaluated, it may be changed at the discretion of the store personnel. Each student may also be assigned a partial grade based on the appearance of the entire store at the end of the display team effort.

FIGURE 15–14 *The pyramid on platform vase with plexiglas envelope display. Relate high fashion with products in use.*

DISPLAY CONSTRUCTION CHECK LIST

1. Decide on merchandise to be displayed.   ————————
2. Select display area.   ————————
3. Fill in display sketch sheet.   ————————
4. Lay out the showcard.   ————————
5. Produce the showcard.   ————————
6. Arrange to obtain merchandise (use Loan Sheet if necessary).   ————————
7. Clean and prepare display area.   ————————
8. Accumulate props.   ————————
9. Put the display in the display area.
10. Evaluate the display (use Evaluation Sheet).   ————————
11. Return merchandise.   ————————
12. Return props.   ————————
13. Clean display area.   ————————
14. File materials on display in project packet for use in final portfolio.   ————————

SKETCH SHEET

Name _____

Name _____

Name _____

Sketch # _____
(Display Area #)

S K E T C H

Materials from Lab: _____ (Numbers)

_____ (Numbers)

_____ (Numbers)

Outside of lab materials: _____

Merchandise: _____

Showcard theme: (Actual words to appear on card)

_____

Signature of Instructor:

_____

DISPLAY EVALUATION SHEET

Criteria	Possible Points	Points	Comments
Subject—Its appropriateness in the store situation	10		
Neatness and preparation of the display area	5		
Message and total effect	5		
Elements: Props Shelf Lighting Showcard Merchandise	10		
Organization and planning: Promptness Sketch	5		
Principles: Emphasis Harmony Balance Rhythm Proportion	10		
Color—Theme and execution	5		

MERCHANDISING/PROP LOAN SHEET

The Visual Merchandising class at _____ School is in the process of constructing displays as part of their class activities. The students will be able to practice the various visual merchandising principles, procedures, and techniques better if they have a variety of display projects. Therefore, please loan them the materials as explained in the attached Project Sheet.

The student has the responsibility of caring for, using, and returning all of the materials. However, please understand that they will be used in actual displays.

Thank you again for assisting the student in receiving a practical learning experience.

Sincerely,

_____

Instructor's Name

16

Lettering and Sign Layout

SIGN LAYOUT

Guidelines that might be discussed concerning effective sign layout are many and varied. Below are a few of the most common principles. You will master variations on the principles and additional techniques as you progress in lettering skill.

Special attention should be given to sign and showcard margins. The left and right margins should be exactly equal and usually should not exceed two to three inches. The top margin should be approximately one to one and a half times the size of the side margins. The bottom margin should be the largest, twice the size of the side margins and one and a half times the size of the top margin.

The focal point of a sign should appear near the optical center of the sign, which is exactly halfway between the left and right margins and slightly above the top-to-bottom midpoint. Letters and words will obviously be seen and read from left to right. The same principles of proportion, balance, and emphasis discussed in the preceding chapters should be used when laying out a sign.

In producing a showcard, line borders are often used to contain the eye. These lines, which may extend completely around the sign or appear only in defining its corners, should stay within the prescribed margins suggested above. They often add a completed and professional appearance to the sign and may be added to balance the contents of the sign if necessary.

Showcards, a necessary part of any display area, are most impressive and effective when produced individually by the person creating the display, so that their layout, lettering style, and total effect are in keeping with the mood of the display.

As display persons' lettering skill increases, their showcards will reflect their creativity and imagination. Therefore, more restricting rules of lettering will not be set forth here.

PRINCIPLES OF LAYOUT

In lettering, *layout* means the arrangement of copy, designs, or illustrations on a showcard.[1] Layout is very important to the success of a showcard. Even though the lettering may be perfect, if your layout is not harmonious, your card will lack *visual impact*.

[1]This section adapted from "Principles of Layout," *Lettering & Layout Techniques* (Madison, Wis.: Board of Vocational, Technical & Adult Education, 1963), p. 24.

The two usual types of layout are formal (symmetrical) and informal (off-centered or asymmetrical). If a line were drawn through the center of a formal layout, both sides would be equal. If this were done to an informal layout, the sides would not be equal in either amount or size of copy, design, or illustrations. But the informal layout would balance visually, owing to the placement of contrasting sizes, shapes, colors, lines, and so on.

To understand why this balance would exist, imagine a seesaw, with a child at each end. If the children are of the same weight (formal layout), the seesaw will balance. If they are not of the same weight (informal layout), one child must move closer to or farther from the center of the seesaw. The same principle applies to the placement of elements within an informal layout.

Formal layout is the easier of the two to master. For this reason, our first exercise concerns the problem of laying out a sign for homogenized milk, which follows. Before doing this, we must consider the rules for margins and optical centers.

Margin Rules. The margin numbers represent units or proportions. For example, if you used a quarter of an inch as the unit, the sides would be one inch (four units), the top one and a quarter inches (five units), and the bottom one and three-quarter inches (seven units), as in Figure 16−1. Try to maintain as much white space as possible around the copy.

The Optical Center. The optical center is one-tenth the distance above the true center (Figure 16−2). The eye will usually make contact with this portion of the card first. Therefore, use this center to good advantage. Place in this area the important heading that will catch the viewer's attention.

STEPS IN LAYOUT

Let's assume a local grocer has asked you to make a card, 11″ × 14″, vertical. The copy reads as follows: Homogenized Milk, 1 gallon, $1.87.

First Step: The copy is received. At this point, valuable information can be obtained from the copy writer, such as preferred colors, where the copy is to be placed, what are felt to be the most important elements, and if the card requires an easel.

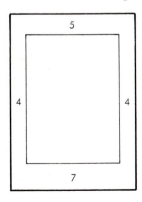

FIGURE 16−1

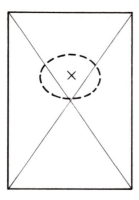

FIGURE 16–2

Second Step: Rank the importance of words or elements by numbers or letters; for example:

(4)
Homogenized
(1)
Milk
(3)
1 gallon
(2)
$1.87

Third Step: Make thumbnail sketches of these elements, and choose the best layout for transfer to the showcard. These sketches should be made in proportion to the finished card. In each sketch, attempt a different approach, until an effective layout is created. See Figure 16–3.

Fourth Step: Begin drawing guidelines for the best sketch on your card.

Fifth Step: Begin inking, starting at the top line to the left. Working to the right, move down to the second line of copy, and repeat the process. Use a variety of sizes to give the card contrast in weights of words. Avoid the monotony of using the same size of pen all the way through.

FIGURE 16–3

Sixth Step: When the sign is thoroughly dry, clean off pencil marks with an art gum eraser (optional if guidelines are light, since erasers streak some showcards). See Figure 16−4.

LAYOUT PRINCIPLES AS RELATED TO DESIGN PRINCIPLES

As we have said, the principles of layout are directly related to the general principles of design: balance, proportion, dominance (contrast), and the direction of attention through suggested movement.

Balance. The two kinds of balance are *formal* and *informal*. Figure 16−5 illustrates them and shows examples.

Proportion. *Proportion* refers to the relation of the parts to each other. It is achieved through *variety, color, line,* and *type*. Proportion is essential to attractive cards. See Figure 16−6.

Dominance and Subordination. Some parts of the layout should stand out on the card. This can be achieved by giving a larger area to some particular part of the copy.

Dominance may also be obtained through interesting lines, strong contrasts, white space, odd shapes, or colors. See Figure 16−7 for examples.

Lines of Direction (Suggested Movement). Figure 16−8 illustrates some of the ways movement can be suggested to lead the eye in the desired direction.

EXAMPLES OF INFORMAL LAYOUT

Informal layouts are most effective in attracting attention, directing eye flow, and providing variety to your showcards. The examples in Figure 16−9 illustrate several techniques in achieving such layouts.

CONCLUSIONS ON LAYOUT

As you can see, there are no set rules in layout beyond the basic principles of design. Your best approach is to study many forms of layout to see what seems to work best, making sketches along the way. Keep in mind that you must have a reason for what you

FIGURE 16−4

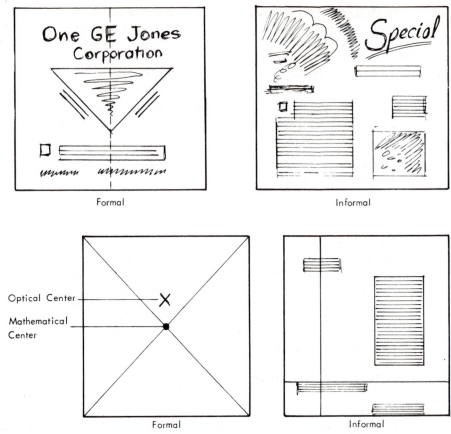

Formal   Informal

Formal   Informal

FIGURE 16-5

do, and then analyze what you have done to determine whether you have accomplished that goal.

HAND/COIT LETTERING TECHNIQUES

INTRODUCTION

An appropriate sign must be included in each display so that the promotional message is effective. The method of lettering to be described below will enable the student to produce professional signs for displays. With concentrated effort, individual practice, and some instructor aid as you begin, you will master the alphabet easily. It is an inexpensive and often highly stylized method of producing showcards for displays.

If the display student prefers, he or she may use other methods of sign production if the school or store has special equipment or makes it available. These additional sign production methods include the Varigraph, sign presses, any number of sign machines and sign production kits, stencils, and press type.

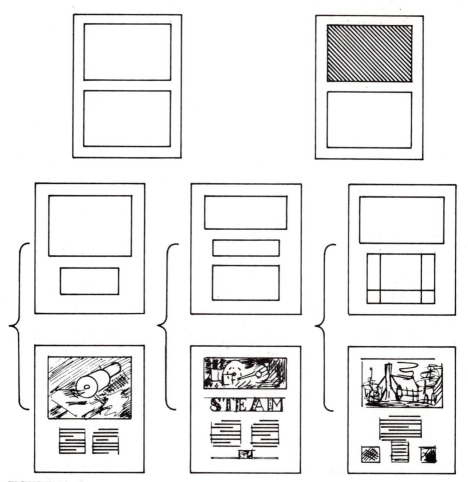

FIGURE 16−6

SHOWCARD LETTERING PROCEDURES

The creation of effective showcards for the display window is an integral part of display production, since the showcard is one of a display's five elements. Showcards may be most easily created by using watercolor tempera paints in a proportion of three parts of paint to two parts of water and/or undiluted India ink. Other media may be used, but these two items are most accessible and most easily utilized by the display person. Eight-ply showcards are most adaptable for use in the production of a sign. Magic Markers and like equipment may be used to decorate, border, and otherwise enhance a sign, but never to produce letters.

For the display person to lay out a showcard easily, the use of guide sticks is suggested. These are long, straight sticks constructed of one-eighth- to one-quarter-inch nonflexible materials. They are cut in varying widths and used in proportion to the varying widths of lettering pens. Lines are drawn on either side of the guide stick,

Strong Contrast
in Size or Color

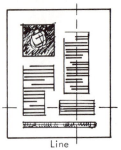

Line

Interesting Lines

White Space

Odd Shapes

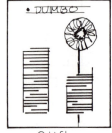

Odd Shapes

FIGURE 16-7

FIGURE 16-8

"Cabbage today only" balances
"2 pounds 39 cents"

"Attention" and the dot above
it balance the rest of the layout

Diagonal balance — "Rugs" balances
the rest of the copy

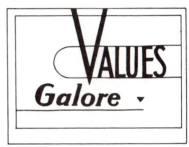

Another diagonal balance

FIGURE 16—9

giving the artist top and bottom border lines within which to construct the letters.

The widths of guide sticks used with different pen widths are as follows:

⅜-inch pen point with a 2¼-inch guide stick

½-inch pen point with a 3-inch guide stick

1-inch pen point with a 5-inch guide stick.

Letters should be one and a quarter to one and a half inches in width and should be drawn as close together as possible without touching each other. There should be a distance of approximately three finger widths between words when using a ⅜-inch pen, or a width of one and one half letters when using other width pens.

The Coit pen, which is the kind most often used in this type of showcard production, should be held at a 45-degree angle, regardless of the direction of the stroke.

Trial strokes should be made until pen control is mastered and the pen is distributing its ink evenly and precisely. If the ink flow is unsatisfactory, the pen point should be reset and cleaned with water and abrasive cleanser, and the paint or ink mixture reexamined.

The tip of the pen point must be kept in contact with the paper at all times while completing a stroke. With a full wrist and arm movement, *pull, do not push the pen,* working fast enough to achieve uninterrupted flowing strokes in the production of a letter. Do not restroke letters.

When coming to the end of a stroke, slow up the speed with which you are lettering. Pause an instant at the end of each pen stroke before lifting the pen from the card, to avoid blotting.

To summarize showcard lettering:

1. *Materials needed:*
    a. Coit pens - ⅜", ¼", ½"
    b. Two empty bottles
    c. Two Magic Markers
    d. Poster paper
    e. Poster board
    f. Guide sticks
    g. Paint
    h. Ink
2. *Procedure:*
    a. Mix showcard paint—3 parts paint and 2 parts water, or use undiluted India ink.
    b. Fill one bottle with water and one bottle with paint or ink.
    c. Select Coit pen and corresponding guide stick:

Pen	Guide Stick
⅜"	2¼"
½"	3"
2"	5"
¼"	5"
	1¼"

    d. Make trial strokes on paper to get pen running.
    e. Make guide lines on paper.
3. *Rules:*
    a. Keep the tip of the pen point in full contact with the paper.
    b. Hold the Coit pen at a 45° angle.
    c. With a full wrist and arm movement, *pull*, do not push, the pen. Complete each stroke. Work directly in front of your body.
    d. Letters should be uniform in width.
    e. Letters should be as close to each other as possible (no more than ¼ inch apart).

f. For the Coit alphabet used in class, letters should slant slightly from upper left to lower right.

g. Pause a moment at the end of each stroke before lifting the pen from the paper.

h. Master each letter as you go along. Follow the letter sequence suggested in class.

INSTRUCTIONAL SEQUENCE, COIT UPPERCASE

I
1. Be sure to hold your pen at a 45-degree angle to the guidelines.
2. Keep the pen in full contact with the paper and do not hesitate to use moderate pressure.
3. PULL, do not push the pen.
4. Use the entire arm, not just the hand.
5. Watch the slant of the "I." It should move slightly from left to right.
6. Pause momentarily at the end of the stroke before lifting the pen straight up off the paper.
This is a basic stroke and should be perfected before going on.

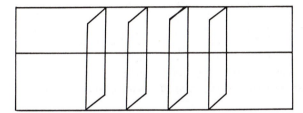

T
1. In making the first stroke (the crossbar of the "T"), hold the pen at the same angle as for the letter "I."
2. Make the stroke, using the entire arm, in one continuous motion. Make the crossbar touch the upper guideline all the way across (approximately 1½ inches).
3. The second stroke is like the letter "I."
Continue to watch the slant of the letter and the 45-degree angle of your pen.

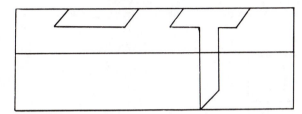

L
1. First draw the letter "I." Then make a stroke like the cross stroke of "T," but placed at the bottom (about 1½ inches).
2. The entire letter is completed without lifting the pen from the paper.

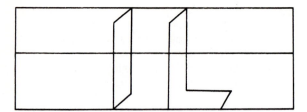

F

1. The first stroke is the same as that for the "I."
2. The second stroke is like that of the top of the "T." Continue to maintain the 45-degree angle on the pen.
3. The third stroke is the same length as the second and is placed just below the midway point of the down stroke.
Always remember to work from left to right and from top to bottom.

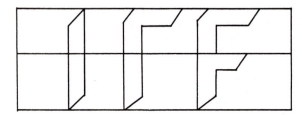

E

1. The letter "E" is similar to the "F."
2. After drawing an "L," complete the "E" in the same manner as the "F."
Remember to keep constant pressure on your pen so that the flow of ink will be uniform.

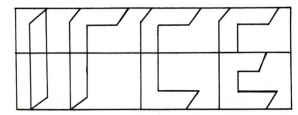

H

1. The "H" is made by first drawing two parallel down strokes like the "I."
2. The third stroke, which joins the two parallel lines, should be placed just below the midpoint.

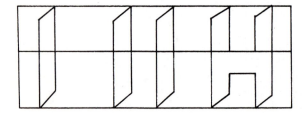

A

1. The first stroke is again the letter "I."
   Note: Lettering sequence is based on progressive steps.
2. Making the second stroke is like drawing an upside down and backwards "L," starting at the top of the first stroke, without lifting the pen.
3. The third stroke is the same as the crossbar used in the letter "H."
   Continue to check the 45-degree angle of the pen by observing consistency in stroke endings.

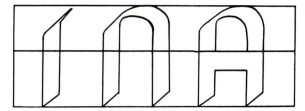

N

1. Two parallel down strokes are drawn as in the "H."
2. The third stroke connects the top of the first stroke with the bottom of the second stroke.
3. Be sure that there is a 45-degree angle at the bottom of the third stroke.
   Check periodically to see that your lettering is slanting slightly from top left to bottom right.

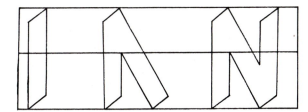

M

1. The "M" will be wider than all previous letters because of the four-stroke construction.
2. The first two strokes are parallel down strokes.
3. The third stroke is similar to the third stroke of the "N" except that this stroke ends slightly past the halfway point between the two vertical lines.
4. The fourth stroke starts at the top of the second stroke and crosses into the third stroke just above the bottom guideline. Note that this stroke violates the left-to-right rule.

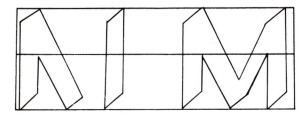

V   1. The "V" is simply made of the third and fourth strokes of the "M."
         2. Watch the ending angle (45 degrees) where the two strokes are joined.

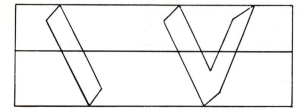

W   1. The "W" is made by drawing two "V's" that are connected at the top in the middle. Like the "M," this letter is wider because of the four strokes used.
         2. Be sure that all the angles where lines are joined are 45 degrees.

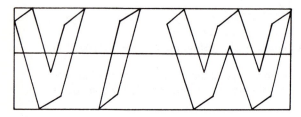

X   1. This letter is made wider at the bottom (1½ inches) than at the top in order to prevent the appearance of instability.
         2. The first stroke is a diagonal drawn left to right, top to bottom.
         3. The second stroke is diagonal drawn right to left and top to bottom. Note that the second stroke, like stroke four of the "M," violates the left-to-right rule.

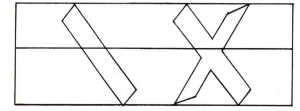

Y   1. The first stroke is similar to the "X," but ends at the midpoint of the guidelines.
         2. The second stroke begins at the upper guideline, meets the first stroke, and then continues straight down to the bottom guideline.

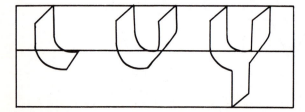

K
1. The first stroke is the letter "I."
2. The second stroke is like the second stroke of the letter "Y," but it is pulled down to the right to complete the letter.
3. The width of the "K" at the base is greater than the width at the top.

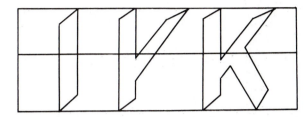

Z
1. The "Z" is one continuous stroke.
2. The top of the letter is made like the top of a "T." The stroke is then completed by PULLING the pen at the 45-degree angle down to the bottom line.
3. The letter is finished by repeating the top stroke of the letter, but along the bottom guideline.
4. The base of the "Z" should be slightly to the right of the top to prevent the appearance of tipping.

P
1. Again, the first stroke is the "I."
2. The second stroke starts at the top of the first stroke and is slowly pulled down in the shape of a half-moon to a point just below in the middle of the space between guidelines.
3. The third stroke starts just below the midpoint of the "I" and is drawn across the paper into the second stroke.
4. Note the 45-degree angle where the second and third strokes join.

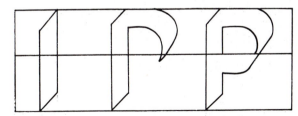

B
1. The first two strokes are like the first two strokes of the letter "P."
2. The third stroke is similar to the second stroke in the "P," and is pulled down into another half-moon which just touches the bottom guideline.

3. The fourth stroke is like the third stroke of the "P," joining the bottom of the "I" with stroke three.
Again note 45-degree angles to test consistency in letter construction.

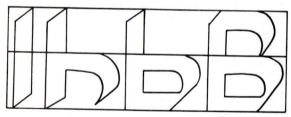

R
1. The first three strokes are the same as the letter "P."
2. The fourth stroke is a short diagonal beginning just to the left of the intersection of the second and third strokes. It is pulled down to the right to complete the letter.

D
1. The first stroke is the letter "I."
2. The second stroke is a large half-moon drawn from the top of the "I" and pulled down to touch the bottom guideline.
3. The third stroke is pulled along the bottom guideline, left to right from the "I," and slipped into the second stroke.

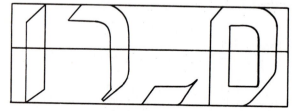

C
1. The first stroke is started slightly below the top guideline and is pulled down and slightly to the left at first, then straight down until the base is reached.
2. Without lifting the pen, construct the base by pulling the pen sideways in a looping action and sliding the pen slightly upward. The base takes on the appearance of a rocking chair.
3. The second stroke places a small half-moon on the top of the "C."

G 1. The first stroke is like that of the letter "C."
2. The second stroke starts slightly below the midpoint of the guidelines. It is pulled to the right and down to the left, into the end of the first stroke. Note the corner effect in the second stroke.
3. The third stroke is the same as in the second stroke in the letter "C."

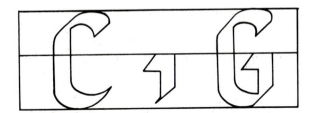

O,Q 1. The first stroke is like that of the letter "C."
2. The second stroke is the first stroke in an upside down and reversed position.
3. Note the 45-degree angle where the two strokes are joined at the top and bottom.
4. This letter is not round, but instead has two flat sides and a slightly rounded base and top.

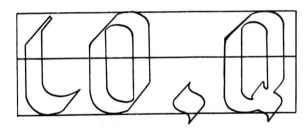

5. The first two strokes are the same as for the letter "O."
6. The third stroke is a short diagonal starting in the middle of the base of the "O" and continuing below the guideline.

U 1. The first stroke of the "U" starts like the "I" but is completed in a fashion similar to the first stroke of the "O."
2. The second stroke is like the "I" but slides left into the first stroke at the base.

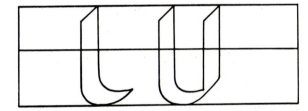

J 1. The first stroke is similar to the base of the first stroke in the "U."
2. The second stroke repeats the second stroke of the "U."

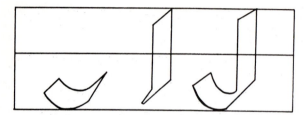

S
1. The first stroke starts at the top of the paper, is curved downwards, then to the right, and then slightly to the left.
2. The second stroke completes the bottom loop, starting a third of the way up the paper and curving to the right and into the first stroke.
3. The third stroke is like the second stroke of the "C."

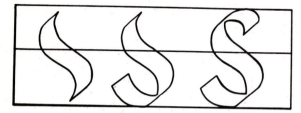

?
1. The first stroke is like the beginning of the first stroke of the letter "S."
2. The second stroke starts at the top, touching the first stroke, curving along the top, down to the left, then back to the right to the bottom of the space, ending on a point.
3. The third stroke is the period.

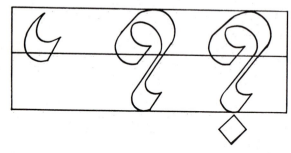

" ",-
1. Quotation marks are short, curved strokes and are placed about one third of the way down in the space.
2. The hyphen is made with one short stroke, slightly below the midpoint of the space.

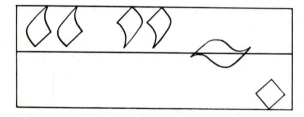

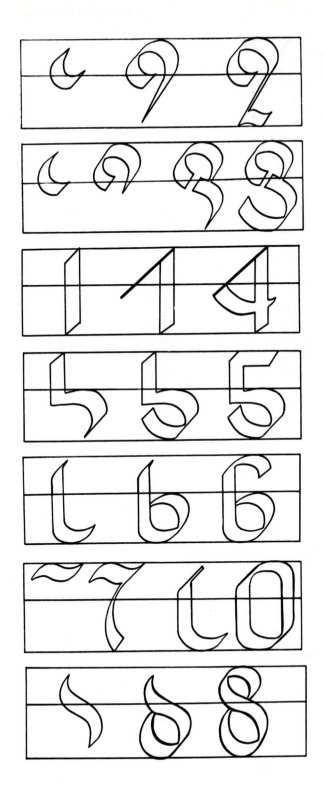

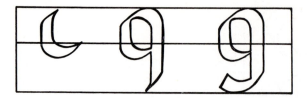

Project Twelve: ON-THE-JOB DISPLAY CONSTRUCTION

This project is for the student who has obtained a position in a retail store as the store display person. In smaller stores, this may be a part-time position. Displays created in the store by the student may be evaluated by student and instructor through appointment.

A different area of the store may be used each time the student is able to substitute or supplement a store display for an in-class activity. The areas should follow a pattern that will take the student from a simple case or shadow-box display to an exterior window and eventually to a total display effort involving several areas.

Depending on the type and scope of merchandise handled by the store, these in-store projects may involve up to one-half the student's display assignments, but they should not be a substitute for nondisplay classroom evaluations, demonstrations, and so on.

DISPLAY CONSTRUCTION CHECK LIST

1. Decide on merchandise to be displayed.   _____
2. Select display area.   _____
3. Fill in display sketch sheet.   _____
4. Lay out the showcard.   _____
5. Produce the showcard.   _____
6. Arrange to obtain merchandise (use Loan
   Sheet if necessary).   _____
7. Clean and prepare display area.   _____
8. Accumulate props.   _____
9. Put the display in the display area.
10. Evaluate the display (use Evaluation Sheet).   _____
11. Return merchandise.   _____
12. Return props.   _____
13. Clean display area.   _____
14. File materials on display in project packet for use
    in final portfolio.   _____

SKETCH SHEET

Name _____

Name _____

Name _____

Sketch # _____

(Display Area #)

S K E T C H

Materials from Lab: _____ (Numbers)

_____ (Numbers)

_____ (Numbers)

Outside of lab materials: _____

Merchandise: _____

Showcard theme: (Actual words to appear on card)

_____

Signature of Instructor:

_____

Project Thirteen: DISPLAY INTERNSHIP

This project is intended to give the student display experience as a member of a real display team, so that prop preparation, display schedules, timing, and merchandise selection will become more meaningful.

Any student who desires to have additional display experience in lieu of, or in addition to, constructing a display may wish to arrange a visitation day with the display department of a major department store.

DISPLAY EVALUATION SHEET

Criteria	Possible Points	Points	Comments
Subject—Its appropriateness in the store situation	10		
Neatness and preparation of the display area	5		
Message and total effect	5		
Elements: Props Shelf Lighting Showcard Merchandise	10		
Organization and planning: Promptness Sketch	5		
Principles: Emphasis Harmony Balance Rhythm Proportion	10		
Color—Theme and execution	5		

MERCHANDISING/PROP LOAN SHEET

The Visual Merchandising class at _____ School is in the process of constructing displays as part of their class activities. The students will be able to practice the various visual merchandising principles, procedures, and techniques better if they have a variety of display projects. Therefore, please loan them the materials as explained in the attached Project Sheet.

The student has the responsibility of caring for, using, and returning all of the materials. However, please understand that they will be used in actual displays.

Thank you again for assisting the student in receiving a practical learning experience.

Sincerely,

_____

Instructor's Name

Criteria involved in this arrangement include correspondence indicating that the store is expecting the student and that the student will be able to participate fully with the store's display team for an entire day. The activity that will dominate the visitation day must be described as to whether it will involve scheduling, prop preparation, changing of displays, or merchandise selection and preparation.

The student, upon returning from this display experience, will give an oral report to other class members, describing the activities, and will either submit a written report of these activities to the instructor for evaluation or arrange for an in-depth evaluation interview with the instructor.

17

Supplemental Alphabets

LOWERCASE COIT ALPHABET

LETTERS WITH SERIFS

1. Draw three parallel guidelines, with the space between the top two lines slightly smaller than the space between the bottom two.
2. Holding the pen at a 45° angle, start the stroke at the middle guideline for the smaller letters, or at the top guideline for the taller letters, such as *b* and *h*.
3. Slide the pen horizontally for ¼ inch, then stop. This top edge of the letter is called a serif.
4. Do not lift the pen from the paper.
5. With locked wrist, pull the pen downward.
6. At the bottom of the stroke, curve the pen slightly upward. (You may wish to release pressure on the pen while doing this.)
7. Check to see that the bottom right edge of the letter is parallel with the top left edge.
8. For letters that extend below the line—*g, j, p, q, y*—draw a fourth guideline, the same distance below the third as that between the second and third lines.
9. Begin the first stroke at the second guideline from the top.
10. For all except *p* and *q*, extend the second stroke to a point one-half the distance between the bottom two guidelines.
11. Holding the pen at a 45° angle, slide the pen on its narrow edge to the left half an inch.
12. Begin the left edge of the third (bottom) stroke parallel to the left edge of the first stroke, and curve the third stroke to join the second.
13. The bottoms of the *p* and *q* are made like the bottom of th *i*.

LETTERS WITHOUT SERIFS

1. Do not slide the pen horizontally to the right at the top of vertical strokes.
2. Pull the stroke directly downward for all vertical strokes.
3. Do not curve the stroke upward at the end of vertical strokes (with the exception of the *t*).
4. Curved letters such as *o, c, x, e, s*, and *g* are made the same way in all cases.

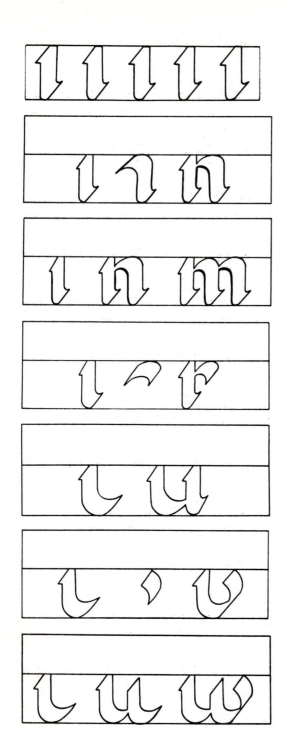

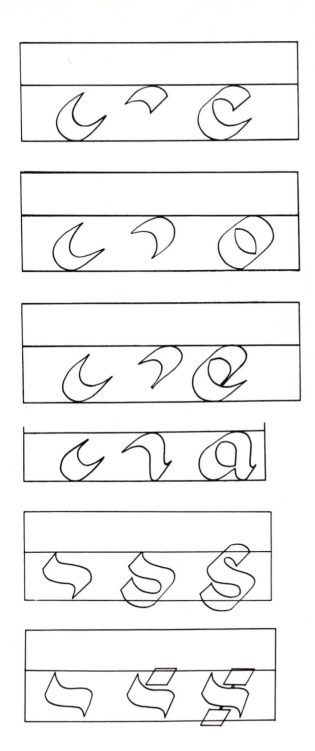

205

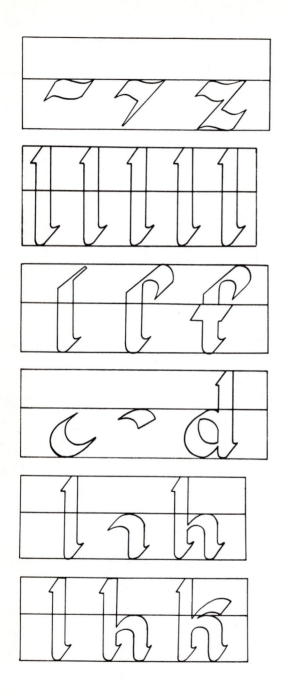

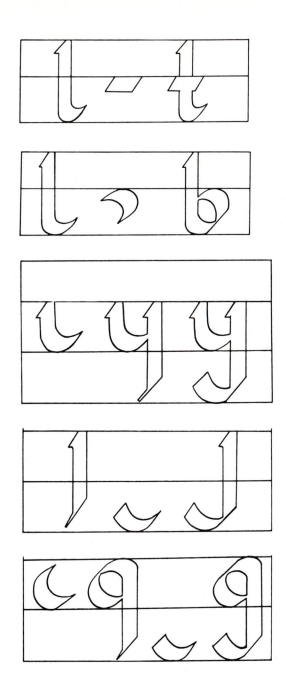

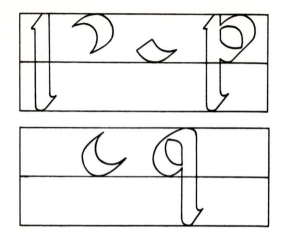

him
and
her

abcd
their
folly

OTHER TYPES OF ALPHABETS

The following types of alphabets can be produced using the principles set forth in the previous pages.

ABCDEFGH

IJKLMNOPQR

STUVWXYZ

Uppercase Old English

abcdefghij

klmnopqrs

tuvwxyz

Lowercase Old English

210

ABCDEF
GHIJKLM
NOPQRST
UVWXYZ
abcdefghijklmno
pqrstuvwxyz &
1234567890

ABCDE
FGHIJK
LMNOP
QRSTU
VWXYZ
123456789

ABCDEFG
HIJRLMN
OPQRSTU
VWXYZ &
abcdefghijklmno
pqrstuvwxyz
123456789

ABCDEF
GHIJKL
MNOPQR
STUVWX
Flat-nib YZ *Script*
abcdefghij
klmnopqr
stuvwxyz

Style variations

211

18

Sources
of Information
and Material

bibliography
glossary

BIBLIOGRAHY

Allphin, Willard, *Primer of Lamps & Lighting*. Philadelphia: Chilton Company, 1962.

Aloi, Robert, *Esposizioni*. Cincinnati, O.: Display Publishing Company, 1962.

Benson, John Howard, and Arthur Graham, *The Elements of Lettering*. New York: McGraw-Hill, 1960.

Bernard, Frank J., *Dynamic Display*. Cincinnati, O.: Display Publishing Company, 1962.

——, *Dynamic Display Technique and Practice*. Cincinnati, O.: Display Publishing Company, 1966.

Buckley, Jim, *The Drama of Display—Visual Merchandising & Its Techniques*. New York: Pellegrini & Cudahy.

Buzan, Lloyd, *Rigging and Forming Men's Wear for Display*. Cincinnati, O.: Display Publishing Company, 1962.

Castro, Nestor, *The Handbook of Window Display*. New York: Architectural Book Publishing Company, 1958.

Coffin, Harry B., *Art Archives*. New York: Art Archives Press, 1964.

——, *Designs, Borders, Backgrounds, Tints, & Patterns*. New York: Studio-Cromwell.

Curtis, Freida, *How to Give a Fashion Show*. New York: Fairchild Publications, Inc.

Davis, Deering, *Contemporary Decor*. New York: Architectural Book Publishing Company.

Elliott, Charles B., *Pointers on Display*. Washington, D.C.: Small Marketers Aids, Small Business Administration, 1969.

Fashion & Research Staffs of Women's Wear Daily, *Fifty Years of Fashion*. New York: Fairchild Publications, Inc., 1974.

Fernandez, Jose Antonio, *The Specialty Shop*. New York: Architectural Book Publishing Company, 1950.

Franck, Klaus, *Exhibitions*. New York: Praeger, 1961.

Gaba, Lester, *The Art of Window Display*. New York: Studio-Cromwell.

Gardner, James, and Caroline Heller, *Exhibition and Display*. New York: F.W. Dodge Corporation, 1965.

Graves, Maitland, *The Art of Color and Design*. New York: McGraw-Hill, 1968.

Herdig, Walter, *Window Display*. New York: Praeger, 1961.

Hotchett, Melvin S., *Merchandise Display*. Austin: University of Texas Press, 1972.

Kasper, Karl, *Shop and Showrooms*. New York: Praeger, 1967.

Koeninger, Jimmy G., *You Be the Judge: Display*. Columbus, O.: Ohio Distributive Education Materials Laboratory.

Lehmann, J. N., *Promotion of Home Goods*. Los Angeles: Manlay Publishing Company.

Lehner, Ernst, *Alphabets and Ornaments*. New York: Museum Books, Inc.

Lichten, Frances, *Decorative Art of Victoria's Era*. New York: Scribner's.

Matteson, Michael T., Roger N. Blakeney, and Donald R. Domm, *Contemporary Personnel Management*. San Francisco: Canfield Press, 1972.

Mauger, Emily M., *Modern Display Techniques*. New York: Fairchild Publications, Inc., 1969.

Minsky, Betty Jane, *Gimmicks Make Money in Retailing*. New York: Fairchild Publications, Inc.

Nelson, George, *Display*. New York: Whitney Publications, Inc., 1968.

Nicholson, Emrich, *Contemporary Shops in the United States*. New York: Architectural Book Publishing Company.

Parnes, Louis, *Planning Stores That Pay*. New York: F.W. Dodge Corporation.

Payne, George, *Creative Display*. New York: National Retail Merchants Association, 1962.

Principles of Merchandising Display & Principles of Merchandise Display Workbook. Austin: University of Texas, Distributive Education Division.

Rowe, Frank A., *Display Fundamentals*. Cincinnati, O.: Display World (Dept DF), 1962.

Samson, Harland E., and Wayne G. Little, *Display, Planning and Techniques*. Cincinnati, O.: South-Western Publishing Co., 1979.

Show Card Lettering. Madison: Wisconsin State Board of Vocational and Adult Education, 1963.

Small Marketers Aid No. 63—Making the Most of Your Show Windows. Washington, D.C.: Small Business Administration, 1970.

Store Lighting—Interior and Exterior. New York: Illuminating Engineering Society.

Stores. New York: National Retail Merchant Association Publishers, 1980.

Valenti, G.M., *Interior Display: A Way To Increase Sales*. Washington, D.C.: Small Business Administration, 1969.

GLOSSARY

Achromatic: Describing neutral colors such as black, white, or grays. They are either totally reflective or totally absorbent of light.

Analogous: Describes a color scheme that consists of from three to five or more different hues, placed consecutively on the color wheel and including no more than one-third of the wheel.

Angled front: Store window that parallels the sidewalk but angles away from the sidewalk contour.

Arcade front: Store window and frontage type, very open in sweep.

Asymmetry: Lack of similarity of two sides of a display. Provides an interrelationship of parts to form an esthetically pleasing whole.

Atmosphere lighting: Lighting that plays light against shadow to create a distinctive effect in specific displays.

Balance: Artistically defined as the state of equipoise between the totals of the two sides of an entity.

Black-light displays: Displays in which ultraviolet fluorescent lamps are used in areas of reduced general light level.

Boutique: A small shop selling accessories and separates.

Chroma: Degree of saturation.

Chromatic: Describing colors such as red, yellow, and blue, whose color or hue is due to their respective reflective properties.

Closed-background window: Windows that are shut off from the store completely by partitions.

Color: The presence of light as it is reflected from the surface of an object.

Complementary: Describing a color scheme consisting of two colors or hues that are exactly opposite one another on the color wheel.

Corner windows: On a store front, the central viewing point of converging traffic.

Curved lines: Artistic device, feminine for the most part, and adding flowing movement.

Diagonal lines: Artistic device, may extend from the left side to the right side of a display, thereby creating and inducing action.

Double complementary: Describes a color scheme consisting of four hues, widely separated and appearing on each of the four sides of the color wheel.

Dummy: A shape like a person, used for window and interior display.

Elements of display: Merchandise, shelf or display area, props, lighting, and showcards.

Elevated windows: Store windows that are 12 to 14 inches above the sidewalk.

Elevator windows: Store windows with a floor level that may be raised or lowered at will.

Emphasis: Defined in Webster's as, ''A forcefulness of expression that gives special impressiveness, calls to special attention . . . ; stress . . . given to a certain part or feature. . . .'' In a display, it is the point of initial eye contact.

Fluorescent lighting: System of electrical energy causing phosphors to glow in a tube.

Formal balance: The positioning of each object on the right side of a grouping with an exact counterpart on the left side in regard to size, placement, shape, and color.

Guide sticks: Straight sticks constructed of ⅛″ to ¼″ nonflexible materials cut in varying widths. Used in proportion to varying widths of lettering pens.

Harmony: Agreement between the many parts and aspects of an entity.

Horizontal lines: Lines extending across the surface of an area from one side to the other and terminating at any point in between. Tend to widen the surface on which they are used and seemingly decrease the height of the area.

Hue: Name of a color.

Incandescent lighting: System of electrical energy flowing through a very thin wire filament that resists the flow of energy. This causes it to heat up and glow.

Informal balance: Placement of objects in grouping to achieve component equality by using multiple varieties of object color, placement, size, and shape on opposite sides.

Intensity (in color): Degree of saturation.

Kiosk: An island display in a store that is visible from all four sides, each side having a display placed on it.

Lobby windows: Store windows that follow the lines of deeply recessed entrances.

Mannequin: Lifelike dummy used in stores to display clothing. In French couture terminology, originally referred to live model who wore originals.

Merchandise display: The arrangement and organization of display materials and merchandise to produce a stimulus leading to the sale of merchandise and services by attracting the viewer's attention and inducing action; it is visual selling and acts as a silent salesperson.

Monochromatic: Describing a color scheme that consists of one basic hue, which may appear at any point on the color wheel.

Motif: A main theme or subject to be elaborated on and developed.

Nonpromotional: In display, describes the type of store employing little advertising and few promotional techniques.

Open-back windows: Store windows open to the street-floor area.

Primary lighting: Bare essential of store illumination.

Progression of sizes: Artistic principle of using similar shapes in varying sizes and consistently increasing them in size along the visual path.

Promotional: In display, refers to the store that is committed to a policy of aggressive advertising and promotion.

Proportion: Defined in Webster's as, ''The relation of one part to another or to the whole with respect to magnitude, quantity, or degree. . . . a relation of equality.''

Pyramid: A triangular arrangement culminating at a center peak created by the extension of two equal lines extending from a broad base.

Radiation: In art, either side of a sunburst effect.

Ramped windows: Store windows with elevated floors that form a display area slanted to the front.

Repetition: In display, an artistic device to align items in exactly the same manner as to height, spacing, and the angle at which they are placed.

Repetition of shapes: Similar shapes repeated throughout the display at regular intervals.

Rhythm: In display, the measurement of motion, measure, and proportion culminating in the eventual flow in the entity.

Secondary lighting: In display, spot- and floodlights to augment basic window lighting.

Selling: In display, the five principles of selling are to attract the attention of the passerby, arouse interest, create desire, win confidence, and cause the decision to buy.

Semiclosed-back window: Partitioned store windows extending to a height below the line of vision.

Semipromotional: In display, refers to the type of store that promotes its products, but not vigorously.

Shadow-box windows: In display, small windows inside or outside a store, suitable for small items.

Shape: The visual form of an object.

Size: Physical magnitude, extent, bulk, and dimension of an object.

Split complementary: Describes a color wheel consisting of three hues, one determined as the basic hue in the scheme and the other two appearing on either side of the basic hue's complement.

Step: In display, a level elevation within an area.

Store: Retailing establishment. Stores may be classified as the suburban store, the self-service store, the dealer, and the exclusive shop.

Straight front: Store windows that parallel the sidewalk, with only entrances to break the monotony.

Surrealism: A modern movement in the arts that tries to depict the workings of the subconscious mind.

Symmetry: Interrelationship of parts to form an esthetically pleasing whole.

Texture: In display, the aspect of harmony relating to the sense of touch.

Tone on tone: Describes a color scheme of two hues, next to each other on the color wheel with very little space between them.

Triadic: Describes a color scheme of three colors equidistant from one another on the color wheel.

Value: Refers to a color's range of grays, from white through black.

Vertical line: A line whose direction is from the top to the bottom of a given area. A straight, upright line; when used, it gives a rigid, severe, and masculine quality to an area.

Visual merchandising: Presentation of a store and its merchandise to the customer.

Zigzag: A line based on the principle of the double reverse curve.

Index